Priority
PARENTING

Priority
PARENTING

Reclaiming Your Home
for Heaven's Sake

Steve Ganger

 **Herald Press**
Scottdale, Pennsylvania
Waterloo, Ontario

Library of Congress Cataloging-in-Publication Data
Ganger, Steve.
  Priority parenting : reclaiming your home for heaven's sake / Steve Ganger.
    p. cm.
  Includes bibliographical references (p.   ).
  ISBN 0-8361-9331-8 (pbk. : alk. paper)
  1. Parenting—Religious aspects—Christianity. I. Title.
  BV4845.G36 2006
  248.8'45—dc22

                              2005037768

PRIORITY PARENTING
Copyright © 2006 by Herald Press, Scottdale, Pa. 15683
        Published simultaneously in Canada by Herald Press,
        Waterloo, Ont. N2L 6H7. All rights reserved
Library of Congress Control Number: 2005037768
International Standard Book Number: 0-8361-9331-8
Printed in the United States of America
Cover design by Alison King
Front cover photographs from Stockphoto.com with photos (left to
right) by Galina Barskaya, Dennys Bisogno, and Jeffrey Zavitski.

12 11 10 09 08 07 06   10 9 8 7 6 5 4 3 2 1

To order or request information, please call
1-800-759-4447 (individuals); 1-800-245-7894 (trade).
Web site: www.heraldpress.com

For every parent who has privately wondered if there is
more to family life
(There is.)

Contents

Foreword by Douglas L. Friesen 9
Preface 13

Reclaiming the Home
    1. Heaven's Priority 17
    2. Homesick 33

Empowering the Parent
    3. There's a Spouse in the House 49
    4. Kids Will Say No When You Do. 59

Dethroning the Child
    5. Nobody's Home. 73
    6. Send in the Clouds. 87

Enthroning God
    7. The House of God 97
    8. From Here to Eternity 107

Afterword 117
Notes 119
Bibliography 125
About the Author 127

Foreword

It has become an all too familiar scene in my therapy office: Two parents, sitting together, looking confused and scared. "I thought we were doing what was best for our child," the father might say. "I guess I just wanted her to like me," the mother shares. They are trying to come to grips with a teenager or prepubescent child who is in trouble, perhaps involved in some out of control behavior. And even if the child is not into something quite so serious, the parents are asking me some version of the same question.

"How did things go so awry in our home?" Now they are meeting with me, a psychologist who works with families, to find out how to right the ship in their family. The parents, good caring people, had somehow lost the leadership of their own home. They are now faced with the difficult task of regaining control of a child very much in charge and potentially headed down a painful path.

I recently saw a commercial on television that highlighted the issue of the child running the home. The commercial starts with parents showing astounded looks on their faces opening their cellular phone billing statements. "Who is making all these calls?" they demanded. The commercial then showed children of various ages, some fairly young I might add, talking on cell phones as these parents called to them by their full names. (I always knew I was in trouble when my parents called me using my middle name.) The solution proposed by this commercial? Of course it was an ad for a cell phone company—a family plan that would allow for unlimited family minutes. No limits! Now your child can talk on the cell phone to their heart's content! No limits! No one would dream to suggest that limits be set with the child or teen and if they exceeded these limits, then consequences would be implemented. Setting limits is difficult, and young people have become quite adept at wearing down already overly committed and tired parents. They beg, plead, whine, cry and threaten until they get their way. Children who are used to getting their way don't like limits.

Certainly, parents are not solely to blame for the problems facing children and teens are facing today. Immense pressures from the media and the environment can sway young people negatively. The Internet definitely poses challenges that parents did not face when they were younger.

When I work with children or teens, I do not counsel children in isolation. The parents must be involved. I stress to the parents that *nurture* and *discipline* are the two primary tasks involved in effective parenting. Nurture involves generous doses of love and affection. It is letting the child know that you are on their side and proud of them for whom they are. Discipline or training is letting the child know that, while you love them very much, you want them to know right from wrong, and that there are certain limits to their behavior. Yes, limits. Effective discipline is done in love and is not angry or abusive, but it is clear, consistent, and firm. It lets the child know, even though they may not feel it at the time, that you love them enough to not let them start down a path of self-destructive and damaging behavior.

This is why my friend Steve Ganger's book is so important. Steve boldly goes where other books fall short. This book affirms for parents that it is not okay to allow a child or teenager to run the household. God has given this role to parents, and parents need to not be afraid to be a parent, to be the leader of the home. Even if it means that your child will be upset with you. As the saying goes, they will thank you later. And parents, you will be thankful you read this book and started applying the principles found in the following chapters.

I didn't think it could happen to me. As a therapist I have seen how child-centered families impact marriages. When my wife and I welcomed our son into our family almost one year ago, we were overjoyed. Our time and our energy revolved around him. When we did talk, we usually talked about his care and his latest accomplishments. We loved our son and we worked to provide a loving home for him, but something was missing. Us! We had lost our sense of *us*. With so much energy focused on our son, we stopped working on our relationship and the communication skills so vital to a healthy marriage.

I would like to say that we have figured it all out, but we are still learning. One thing I do know is that we have committed ourselves to making time for each other and not allowing our son, though we love him dearly, to interfere with our marriage. For one of the greatest gifts we can give to him is our love for each other. A stable, healthy, and loving marriage will be very beneficial to his emotional development. It is my hope that this book will challenge parents to love and cherish their children, but to also know when things become out of balance and the child becomes the center of the home. When this happens, efforts need to be made to restore balance and return the home to the leadership of the parents.

—*Douglas L. Friesen, psychologist, pastor, and father*
   Lititz, Pennsylvania

Preface

No family is perfect. No home is without its peculiarities. That is why any book written about family life won't resonate with every in-house dynamic. *Priority Parenting* is no exception.

I want to be sensitive at the start and acknowledge the many single parents who may be reading this book. Over twenty-five percent of children in the U.S. are living in single-parent homes.[1] Though God's ideal is for a two-parent household, single parents face the same challenges as traditional homes, plus many unique ones. It should be noted up front that most of this book has been written from a traditional two-parent perspective, not to be exclusionary, but because the majority of children—nearly two-thirds—live in such a home. Hopefully, single parents will still find the information applicable since *raising* children is a responsibility they share with all fellow parents and guardians, regardless of how many of them are physically in the home.

I also want to remember those readers whose home situations are difficult at best. Many homes are hurting today. Dysfunction is all around. The focus of *Priority Parenting* is not to address those troubled relationships and interpersonal dynamics. That's another book for another author.

If some of the examples or situations shared throughout feel idyllic, they aren't intended as such. There are strong and healthy families, and we need to consider what happens inside those homes as models that call all of us forward in our own families. If anything, troubled families can hopefully take heart and find some encouragement in these pages that a better way is possible. But certainly, the underlying problems won't be solved by reading this book. That's simply not its focus.

The last clarification is that most of the book focuses on parents of preteen children. If you have teenagers in your home, there is still plenty herein that applies to them, but most of the recommendations and examples hone in on families with toddlers, preschoolers, and elementary-aged children.

There is something for everyone, just not *everything* for everyone. That is probably not a surprise to many, but it felt like it needed to be said before you begin reading.

RECLAIMING
THE HOME

1

Heaven's Priority

"I am NOT going to the dentist this morning!" I shouted.

My mother walked over to the hall closet. She must not have heard me.

"I said, 'I am NOT going to the dentist this morning!'"

She began putting on her coat.

I was ten years old, going on four. My lifelong dread of the dentist had driven me to near hysterics. Every year it was the same tired routine. I would barely sleep the night before my checkup, and then when the morning sun broke the horizon, my coup d'état would ensue upon my long-suffering mother.

Except *this* year would be different. This would be the year when my revolt would not be vanquished. This would be the year when the dental chair would sit empty. My mother could drive to the dentist's office if she liked, but I *would not* be riding with her. Victory would be mine.

She picked up her purse, pulled out the car keys, and calmly said as she walked by, "Get your coat. I don't want to be late."

Get my coat? Didn't she hear me? Just who did she think she was?

She was my mother. And she was in charge.

I dejectedly got in the car.

Parents in charge of their children. A novel concept, isn't it? Sadly, in many homes today, it's the other way around. There is a revolution afoot in America—a revolution by children to commandeer the home. And by most accounts, the kids are winning.

We can't really blame them since without a consistent authority structure, children will do what all humans do when left to their own devices—they will try to take control.

Imagine a medieval castle. The king and queen have been summoned to a neighboring kingdom for the day. The royal guard accompanies them, leaving a few tired sentries to watch the castle gate. The royal staff busies themselves with their daily chores. Meanwhile, the prince and princess have the palace to themselves.

What is one of the first things they will do? Exactly. They run to the royal chamber and leap onto mommy and daddy's chairs. They wear their crowns. The prince holds his father's staff and barks out pretend orders. His sister giggles. She lifts a golden goblet and offers an imaginary toast. This is great fun indeed!

One of the royal aides looks in on the commotion and tells the children to desist from their high jinks immediately. The princess laughs and says, imitating her mother's voice, "Leave us alone, grunt! Go check on how the dungeon cleaning is going!" "Better yet," yells the prince, pointing the staff at the aide, "why don't you stay there for the day!" The aide shakes his head and shuts the door. He tells himself, *Thank goodness this is just for one day. The king and queen return in the morning.*

But what if they didn't? What if this wasn't for just one day? What if this is how it would be *every day?* Leaving our make-believe kingdom and looking out upon some twenty-first-century homes, we quickly discover that the fairy tale has come true. In some homes boy kings and girl queens reign, some so small that the royal robe engulfs them like a tidal wave. But reign on high they do, regardless of whether or not you can see their faces underneath the giant crowns.

They rule not so much out of selfish ambition and demands—though those elements certainly exist—but instead, they assume the throne because their parents have relinquished it. Parents have stepped down, some purposely, but most inadvertently. This book is a call to parents to reassume their seats so they can effectively lead their children to healthy relationships with God, their family, their community, and themselves.

In the coming chapters, we will explore God's design for the family and home; examine the roles and role modeling of parents; discuss healthy limits for children and ways to encourage an at-home family dynamic; and recommit to having God-centered families that are focused on eternity, not just on the here and now. Making parenting a priority is not only what is best for parents; it also is what's best for children too.

So why have so many parents allowed their children to take the lead?

The answer is not as complicated as some might expect. It comes down to a basic misunderstanding of God's priority for the home.

Calling the Authorities

Authority? We don't like that word much in our culture. It sounds too oppressive.

Precisely.

Humans have always had a problem with authority. Even though Eve historically has taken the rap for eating the forbidden fruit, it was *Adam* to whom God gave the command.[1] Of course, they *both* disobeyed in the end.[2]

They did what God had specifically told Adam *not* to do. History would show from that point forward that humans do not like being told what to do. Even by God.

But God has told parents what to do in the home: Be in charge. Authorities are God-created, God-designed, and God-ordained. They give order to a created race whose hearts are chronically disordered. Someone needs to be in charge. And God says that *someone* is the parent.

In fact, nowhere in Scripture does God even hint, let alone say, that children should ever be in command. Instead, God directs parents to *lead* and *teach* and *model* for their children a life fully devoted to him.

—To share with children our experience of God's faith-
   fulness (Deuteronomy 4:9)
—To instruct them about God's expectations for how
   we live (Deuteronomy 4:10; 6:7)
—To remind them of what God has said
   (Deuteronomy 11:19; Psalm 78:6)
—To respect and revere our holy God (Psalm 34:11)
—To teach them right from wrong (Deuteronomy 1:39;
   Proverbs 22:6)

And in doing all of this, parents are also reminded that their authority over their children should be with tender love[3] and without unnecessary frustration.[4] For with authority comes great responsibility, and each child is a gift—a blessing, if you will—given by God himself.[5]

In response, the instructions to children are simple and straightforward: to honor, to listen, and to obey their parents.[6]

Easy enough, right?

Of course, do both sides fulfill their roles in the average home? Not always. Certainly not every day. But we stand a better chance of reaching God's ideal when—and only when

—God's authority for the family is adopted.

God has always worked through leadership. The patri-
archs. The judges. The apostles. The pastoral staff. And
yes, the parents.

But it all begins with God. In fact, the leadership that
this book will follow is not just Parent-Child(ren). The full
priority is God-Spouse-Parent-Child(ren). Take a good
look at that list. It begins with God and ends with your
children. This means you fill the gap with responsibilities
to both God and your kids, as well as an ongoing responsibility to your spouse if you are married. This is not an
easy balancing act, but it's clear that God retains his role
on top, and you retain your role of leading your children.

When Moses instructed the people to respect God and
obey his commands for the rest of their lives, he said that
"so you, your children, and your grandchildren. . . ."[7] He
begins with *the parents.* It is their relationship with God
that must take precedence even before their relationship
with their children. In fact, the effectiveness of their relationship with their children is contingent upon a growing
relationship with God *first* (see chapter 3).

God's first commandment is that we would have no
other gods in our life.[8] Only him. And putting children as
our first priority in the name of being a "good parent" is to
deny where our strength and insight ultimately comes from.
I can put my car's engine as the top priority, but unless I fill
the car with gasoline, even the most pristine engine will not
run. The source of the power must come first.

Second, ahead of being a parent in God's priority is the
marriage that created the children in the first place. Being
husbands and wives was intended to supersede being
fathers and mothers. Strong marriages encourage strong
parenting.

Proverbs 22:15 says that every child is filled with

foolishness. Children have many positive qualities too, such as innocence, love and goodwill. But they rely on those who know better and can lead them away from harm and bad decisions.

This makes sense, doesn't it? But we rarely see it anymore. In many families today, the home is centered around children—their needs, their wants, their activities. They call the shots.

The first hint of this rebellion occurs the first time that a toddler says those two ever-present words: "I want. . . ." That is the first crack in the armor of innocence as children begin their journey toward independence. It is their first foray into a "me first" perspective that will always be lurking in the shadows, even as adults. And though they don't say it outright, if allowed, children *want to* be in charge of their lives. The role of the parent is to guide them into that eventual right, but not too soon.

What's Going On?

There is a reason that Fortune 500 companies don't hire twelve-year-olds into executive management (child labor laws aside). A twelve-year-old, no matter how bright, is not mature enough to handle the multiple responsibilities and pressures that come with such a job (they couldn't even drive a rental car on a business trip). A pro football team doesn't draft a nine-year-old Punt, Pass and Kick standout. Their body is only halfway through its natural growth.

Our society has numerous laws to protect children. Curfews, marriage, and school restrictions, age prohibitions for alcohol and tobacco, driver's licenses, and voting rights. No one blinks an eye at these statutes that in effect say, "You're not ready yet. You're too young." So why do we have such a problem in the home? As I said earlier, parents have abdicated their leadership and let their children wreak havoc. But why?

The reasons are complex and many. Here, though, is a partial list of possibilities, including several that will be explored further in the coming chapters.

1. Parents are gone. An empty chair means someone eventually will sit on it. And if parents aren't there, it's easy to see who takes over. Today in America, over one-third of school-age children spend part of the workweek on their own.[9] Over half of all married couples with children see both spouses working.[10] And the number of hours worked has increased significantly—over 160 extra hours per year, which is the equivalent of an extra month.[11]

This is not intended to malign working parents. Tough choices are made every day in this arena. But we cannot ignore the potential ramifications of frequently being away from our children. Being a parent means being there with your children. In fact, the word *parent* is derived from the Latin word that means "to give birth to." A parent is there from the start to nurture and guide.

Imagine being on a guided nature hike through a dense mountain forest. Two miles up the trail, your seasoned guide turns and says to the group, "Okay, folks, I have to run some errands now. Just keep following the path. Watch out for any signs of bears or cougars. Don't eat the dark red berries. And have your rain gear ready. Those clouds look like they could dump at any moment. I'll be back tomorrow. You'll be fine." And then she leaves.

Parents are not occasional tour guides. Parents are along for the entire trek up—*and down*—the mountain of life, . . . no matter what.

Brennan Manning tells the story of three young boys in a daycare facility waiting to be picked up at the end of the day. One boy is bragging that his father is a well-known surgeon who saves lives. Another boy brags that his father is an international lawyer who travels all over the world. The third boy, upon seeing his father enter the room, exclaims, "My daddy is *here!*"[12]

Interestingly, a recent survey of parents and their teenagers found that seventy percent of parents feel they do not spend enough time with their kids, and teenagers cited their top concern as "not having enough time with their parents."[13] Sounds like everybody is thinking the same thing, but no one is doing anything about it.

Parenting was meant for adults. Parents need to consistently give priority to this vocation. Not just for authoritative purposes, but simply because their kids need them to be there. It's what parenthood is all about.

2. Parents want to be their child's friend. If you watch movies, you'll quickly find that "cool" parents are the ones who bend (or abolish) the rules and join their children in pranks and buffoonery. Recall the opening scene from *Mrs. Doubtfire*. It is a birthday party that had wild animals, loud music, and kids running mayhem all over the house. And where was Dad (Robin Williams)? Dancing on the coffee table and rapping with the kids. That was a *cool* dad. But when Mom (Sally Field) walked in, the jig was up. It was Field's character that represented a responsible parent, but she was made out to be a stiff prude. It sends a message to kids that if your parents aren't entertaining and fun, then they aren't very good parents.

Parents should be engaged in their children's interests and activities, but they also should leave room for the kid to be a kid and the parent to be a parent. They are never one and the same. A positive example is a father who joins his son and their friends in a game of touch football. A negative example is the same father helping that same group of boys tee-pee a neighbor's house. The former sends the subconscious message: I love you and being in your life. The latter says: I want to be a kid again. The question every parent has to ask when they purposely enter their child's world is: Is this about them, or is it about me? Often times when parents set their responsibilities on the shelf in order to be a hip parent whom all the kids adore, it's about them, not the kids.

As obvious as it is, many parents have bought into this friendship-centered idea. Nowhere does the Bible—or family counselors—encourage this approach. Child development specialist Betty Caldwell says, "One of the myths of parenting is that it is always fun and games, joy and delight."[14] A myth indeed.

Maintaining your place in household leadership means that your decisions may not always be popular with your kids. Being popular has never been part of the job description though. You're not running for public office. You already hold a lifelong term. Besides, Scripture encourages us that when a child is older, they will return to the wisdom you once shared with them.[15] And it is then that your unpopular decisions will reap positive long-term effects. In fact, being a friend to your child is a privilege that comes later in your relationship, not at the start.

3. Parents want to keep conflict at bay. Keep the peace at all costs. It is easier *in the short-term* to look past our children's constant demands and instead laugh and acquiesce. This is a trend that has been growing for decades. Dr. James McNeal notes the changes in how parental responses have changed during the recent past:[16]

—1980: No. "Don't nag me. I know what's best for you."

—1990: Maybe. "All right, I hear you. I'll consider it."

—1995: Yes. "I understand you prefer that. I'll get it when I go shopping if I can find it on sale."

I wonder what could be said about 2006? "Absolutely. Whatever you want. Please don't cause a scene."

Spend a brief period of time in any supermarket or retail outlet, and it won't take long to see this played out in real life. I once saw a little boy in Wal-Mart who, when denied his favorite candy, dropped to the floor in a screaming tantrum that nearly brought down the shelves. I cringed, wondering how his mother would react. Would she yell at him? Would she swat him? Would she give in and toss the candy in the cart? Instead, she kept pushing the cart down the aisle and never even acknowledged his antics. She walked slowly to keep an eye on him, but he never knew it. After a few seconds, realizing no one was paying attention to him, he lifted his head and stopped crying. His mother kept shopping, and he forlornly rejoined her, tail between his legs. If it had been the dentist office, he would have been a kid after my own heart.

Horse people talk about the moment when a horse submits to its trainer. The animal faces its master and, on signal, walks forward. Now, both the horse and the trainer know who is in charge.

Children, unlike horses, are made in the image of God. However, they still need to be trained. Many parents may be surprised to learn that their job *will* often create conflict with their children. Shouts of "No!" or "That's not fair!" are the human equivalent of a horse snorting and stomping its hooves. It is a natural process of pushing the limits and finding out when the limit has been exceeded.

Child consumerism expert Nathan Dungan notes that "giv[ing] your child everything . . . starts to look like a show of misguided love."[17] Kids don't need you to eliminate conflict from your life together. They need you to model how to handle conflict when it inevitably arrives on the scene.

Is it fun? Not usually. Is it necessary? Most definitely. The author of Hebrews notes, "No discipline is enjoyable while it is happening—it is painful! But afterward there will be a quiet harvest of right living for those who are trained in this way."[18] The Bible often says that discipline is a form of love.[19] Exactly. If you didn't love your child, you'd let them run wild.

4. There's no time and energy left to be a parent. It takes time to be a parent, and these days more parents barely have time for parenting. Many parents come home exhausted from their own trials and time challenges. Lewis Grant calls this syndrome "sunset fatigue,"[20] which means that those we love most get us at our very least—emotionally, physically and spiritually. We're just too wiped out to care.

After a long day, having to face the task of dealing with the kids is more than they can absorb. So for many parents, being a parent has fallen down the priority list as work and other obligations take precedence. As one single mom lamented in a time management workshop I led, "I work two jobs and am trying to complete my degree. When is there time to just be a mom?"

For many, the starting point is their own time management and making time for our children by doing less of other things (see chapter 4). We may be surprised to discover what *doesn't* count as "parenting" even though we are physically near our kids (see chapter 5). If we are under so much stress or so overburdened that *being* a parent is impossible because we're already exhausted on every level, then we need to make a firm commitment to lessen that stress and reduce our outside burdens. It's the classic example of how doing less can actually lead to more.

5. Parents assume that it's too late. Now they are in the stop-the-bleeding mode. Many parents know that things have become out of control. Some even admit it. But they can't even begin to think of how this might change. They are sure that it's too late. What's done is done. Now they simply have to guide the child through high school and pray that it all works out.

The guilt that many parents feel is overwhelming. They ascribe each of their children's problems and struggles to their own inferior parenting. In many ways, it's a self-centered perspective. As expert Mary Whelchel assures us, though, "If you stayed home and devoted every minute to your children, they'd still have problems."[21] Whelchel encourages parents to examine *where* their feelings of guilt are originating—from God or from themselves? As she says, "Just because you *feel* guilty, doesn't mean you *are* guilty."

Child development studies haven't always helped in this area. Many experts tell us that who our child is by age three or at least age nine or ten is who they will be for life. There's a subconscious feeling among parents that if Junior has some cracks in the armor by adolescence, then all hope is gone. While there's no denying that formative opinions and personality traits have been formed along the way, nothing is permanent with God. In Christ, we are all new creations.[22]

Whenever you catch yourself saying, "It's just how they are," remember that the truth is, "It's just how they are *now*." Every great athlete had someone who showed them how to throw a curveball, make a reverse layup, or hit a backhand. Even if you and your child aren't hitting on all cylinders *at the moment,* you can still help them make positive changes *for the future.*

You needn't look any further for hope than Franklin Graham, son of legendary evangelist, Billy Graham. Franklin's autobiography, *Rebel with a Cause,* is a classic example that time never runs out with God. Franklin dropped out of boarding school. He was expelled from college for breaking curfew with a young woman. He even described himself at the time as a beer-drinking motorcyclist.

But then he became a Christian at age twenty-two, and the rest is history. During that time, I'm certain that Billy and Ruth Graham didn't throw in the towel on Franklin. There was much consternation, but there was much prayer and confidence in God's power to initiate change too.

It's never too late to recommit yourself as an involved and caring parent. To give up is to give in.

6. The church has not challenged parents with the biblical mandate to lead and teach their children. Many churches have had Sunday morning focuses on families, marriage, and even parenting, but when is the last time that the church looked its members in the eyes and lovingly said, "*Be* a parent."

I've seen sermon series on family advertised in the local newspapers. It's a safe and popular topic for the general public. But few pastors challenge the upside-down nature of the authority structure. Doing that might actually ruffle some feathers. But that is what Scripture tells us—parents are in charge because God says so. The church needs to say so.

We spend millions of dollars each year *taking care* of

the kids while at church—VBS, children's ministry, and mission trips. How much do we spend on *equipping parents* while at home? One of the greatest renewals in congregational life could come when churches embrace heaven's priority and *first* nurture the parents so that they can better nurture the child.

We have support groups for alcoholics, divorcees, widows, and the unemployed. Why not a support group for parents? It's the hardest and most important job in the world. And God has a lot to say about it. So should the church.

Those are some of the reasons why the vocation of parenting has fallen down the priority list. There are others, to be certain. But in the coming chapters, I want you to set all preconceived notions aside and examine your own family and your own heart. Who sits on the throne of your home? Do any of the six reasons just mentioned hit close to home? Are you struggling with one or two of them? If so, take heart. With God all things are possible,[23] and we are now ready to go further in reclaiming your home for heaven's sake. We'll soon look at what constitutes a real home, and then look at your role as a spouse and take on the overcommitment in your schedule.

Then, we'll look deeply into the hurried lifestyle we are passing along to our kids, and look hard at what God really intends childhood to be. Finally, we talk about ideas for making your house a home that truly worships God first, and then close with a powerful reminder that what we do today in the home matters far beyond the here and now; it has implications for all eternity. Hopefully, that road map makes you want to travel the rest of the way. But as we do, keep in mind that from the beginning, God's intended priority has always been God-Spouse-Parent-Child(ren). Perhaps it's time to realign yours.

There is a *Jimmy Neutron* cartoon episode where all the parents in Retroville are captured by the evil Yokian aliens, leaving Jimmy and his friends free to rule the roost. At first the kids are in ecstasy as they find themselves in an adult-free world. They gorge themselves on fries and soda. They run havoc all over the neighborhoods. It's blissful anarchy as the town unravels around them.

But a strange thing happens the next morning. The kids quickly discover that anarchy isn't all it's cracked up to be. No one is there to care for their upset stomachs and multiple injuries. In fact, it's starting to bother the kids that no rules apply. And when no one's listening, they quietly admit that they *miss* their parents. They miss them so much that soon the kids gather their collective wits and energy to travel to the foreign planet and save their parents. They want Mom and Dad back. They want the rules back. They want to be back in a society of security and structure. It feels right.

That's because it is right. It's been God's plan all along.

Discussions Questions

1. How do you react to the word "authority"? Positively or negatively? Why do you think you respond that way?
2. What kind of family leadership did you grow up in? How has this experience influenced you today?
3. With which of the reasons that parents have relinquished their leadership do you most resonate? Avoiding conflict? Too tired at the end of the day?
4. Who leads in your home today? You or your children?

2

Homesick

According to the U.S. Census Bureau, there are over 120 million houses and apartments in the United States.[1] Take a quick glance at our society, though, and it is easy to see that there are not 120 million *homes*.

New neighborhoods and apartment complexes sprawl across the countryside. "For Sale" signs are frequently spotted. Places to live are not an issue. Actually *living* in those places is another story.

The living home is a dying species. Where a house is constructed for shelter, a home is made for a family. And the family is taking a big hit these days.

Disappearing from the home front are the core characteristics that unite and strengthen families: Eating meals together. Talking together. Playing together. Laughing together. Crying together. Sharing faith together. Just being together. The "old hearthstone," according to nineteenth-century author Herman Melville, where "the heart still fondly turns, ignoring the burden of its anxieties and cares."[2] The home is our refuge from a hard world.

It used to be that way, but today's house has quickly become nothing more than a refueling and technology center where frenetic families occasionally check in to snack, shower, surf the Web, and sleep—a suburban version of an extended-stay hotel. Family life now happens between cell phones and inside minivans or SUVs that traverse crosstown to rehearsals, practices, games, concerts, and an unending schedule of extra-home activities. We stay *in* touch. But rarely do we *actually* touch.

The traditional model of family structures that we were taught as children was predicated on the family *regularly being together*. Remember social studies class and the concentric circles that incorporated the nuclear and extended family, plus the community at-large?

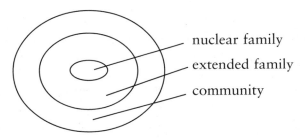

nuclear family

extended family

community

Today, there is no concentricity because no common middle exists. Instead, the nuclear family dissipates into individual units that continuously drift between different groups of people. In essence, today's home is like an asteroid that breaks apart into chunks but occasionally bumps into each other as life's orbit spins them around.

Some argue that such notions are passé. North Americans are no longer a predominantly agricultural society where Pa and Ma run a farm while the kids milk cows and collect eggs. Today, we have cars, computers, MP3 players, and numerous other advancements, so expecting families to be like they were decades ago is unrealistic. I couldn't agree more. I'm not looking for today's families to look and act like the Cleavers. Frankly, I'm just looking for today's families. Where are they? Not in the house, and consequently, not at home.

A House Does Not Make a Home

You may or may not own a house, but you do have a home. We tend to use the words interchangeably, but there are some important differences between them. Consider:

—A house protects from external elements. A home
   protects from internal elements.
—A house is a structure. A home is a structured life.
—A house can be destroyed. A home—good or bad—
   remains forever in the heart.
—A house can be pricey. A home is priceless.

On a golf outing in Kansas City, I played an upscale course in the middle of one of the wealthiest suburbs. Average home prices on the course were over $1 million. Along one of the fairways, I noticed an exotic three-story all-glass house. There were no blinds, so I gawked inside. There was no furniture either.

I commented to one of my playing partners who lived in Kansas City, and he responded, "There are a lot of people like that out here. They can't afford furniture because they spent everything they have on the house."

I met a couple recently who told me that they spent their summer vacation *at their house.* I said, "Why did you do that?" The man smiled wryly and said, "Because it's the one place we've never been together." And he was serious. They had traveled the country, been to every amusement and national park, and all points in between. But they had rarely been at their own house together to experience what that was like. They're not alone.

We have a lot of empty houses today. Some are empty of accessories and furniture. Many are empty of the people who live there. Even more sadly, many are empty of any shred of a home life whatsoever.

What Makes a Home

So what makes a home versus a house? Here are several guidelines for you to consider based on a very simple, unscientific definition: *A home is where the family gathers together regularly.* Let's look at each element.

1. Family. A home exists of and for the family. Now this family can be a nuclear or extended family. It can include friends over for dinner. It can include neighbors and church friends. But it is a family nonetheless, sharing common values and experiences.

I remember as a young teenager sitting in one of my best friend's family rooms. His family was dear to me, and they loved all of his friends who came in the door. But they also were very clear: once inside their home, you were now part of their family. Family rules applied.

While his mom made dinner that night, a friend of ours stood on the couch to change a song on the stereo. A few seconds later, his mom shouted from the kitchen, "Hey, get your feet off that couch right now! You aren't eating at the zoo tonight."

He immediately complied. At first I was a bit stunned. She wasn't our mother. Not biologically, at least. But at that moment, in their home, she *was* our mother. We were part of their family, and there were no perks.

Family means different things to different people, but at its most basic level, it's where we gather with those we love—no matter how that dynamic plays out.

Citing Genesis 22:18, a Spirit-filled Peter reminded the Jews that all the families on earth would be blessed through Abraham's descendants.[3] Family has always been God's idea for all people. And though our true home awaits us in heaven,[4] our earthly family matters greatly to God.

2. Gathers. We gather for a purpose. There is a reason we convene.

Those of you with teenagers or young children in extra-home activities know that gathering is like pulling teeth, but yet it sets a marvelous example. Even though your kids will protest time away from the phone, TV, or computer, they will be learning that some things matter more.

There has been a thirty-three percent decline in families eating together over the last thirty years, despite a well-documented University of Michigan study showing that sharing meals is a leading influence on a child's psychological well-being.[5] According to a recent Urban Institute report, over three million elementary age children regularly take care of themselves without any adult supervision.[6]

Gathering is about much more than food, though. It's a subtle, yet vital way that families remind one another: We're in this together. The classic Three Musketeers battle cry: "One for all and all for one!" It provides a stable reminder that in a tough world, there are people who really care about your welfare.

There is even a spiritual component to gathering. John O'Grady notes that *salvation* "is present when a family sits down at a family celebration in thanksgiving for the goodness they have received and the goodness they contribute to each other."[7] God has always seen our coming together as a *celebration*—of God and each other.

Being together is not just an ideal. It is a divine expectation.

3. Regularly. Special occasions are important, but families must gather on a consistent basis. Make it a common practice. It needs to become an expectation that can be relied upon and fulfilled. A home is a safe place where the hurts of the world are tended. But in order for there to be tending, there needs to be *regular* interaction. If a family is not gathering together regularly, the opportunities for sharing life are squelched, and kids are often left to repress their feelings or share their lives with other kids. Gang experts have noted that the primary reason young men join street gangs is they have no other outlet—no other family in which to share this thing called life.

We all need this connection. Life is hard. We need the support of family to help us through. How many broken hearts roam our streets and fill our pews? Broken because for many years they have had no family upon which to lean consistently. Regularly coming together is not just for crises, but for triumphs, and even the mundane.

But you know what really makes a house a home? That everything I just mentioned happens *inside* the house. That's right. You are actually under the same roof.

At a workshop one afternoon, I shared an alarming statistic about the average amount of talk time between parents and their children today (at the time, it was just under fifteen minutes per day).[8] One man in the audience took immediate exception and interrupted me. "That's not fair," he interjected. "I have great conversations with my kids when we're at the McDonald's drive-through." I couldn't make eye contact with him—half sympathetically and half in shock at what I had heard him say. Many in the room were looking at him in shared dismay. His shoulders quickly sagged as he considered what his statement really said about his home.

He's not alone. Millions of Americans live in houses. Very few are cultivating healthy homes. So why is this happening, and what are some countersolutions for families looking to make their house a home again? It starts with the center of the home.

The Center of the Universe

Our solar system centers on the sun. All nine planets and their moons, along with comets, asteroids, and other space objects, continuously orbit the sun. Everything revolves around it. From ninety-three million miles away, life on earth is sustained from its light and warmth. Some civilizations even worshipped the sun.

Interestingly, many people today live in a family system that centers on the son (or daughter). All activities and special events, along with conversations, sharing, and togetherness, continuously orbit the son or daughter. Everything revolves around them. Life at home is sustained from their light and warmth. Some families even worship the son or daughter (more on that later).

That's what good parents do though, right? They put their kids' welfare, interests, and dreams ahead of their own? Absolutely. They make their children the center of the universe—their home life? Not exactly.

I vividly remember the morning when my firstborn son was laid in my arms by an attending nurse in the delivery room. I nearly dropped him because I was expecting nine pounds to feel like ninety. He laid quietly in the crook of my arm, wrapped in a towel, sleeping soundly beneath his miniature stocking cap. I studied his face, marveling at God's attention to detail. I felt his tiny rib cage rise and fall with each breath. I closed my eyes and quietly praised God for the miracle of life, tears of joy welling up.

Time seemed to stand still. It was a moment unlike any other—as if everything I had ever done in my life up until then faded into the distance. Nothing could compare or compete with it. It was the closest to heaven-on-earth that we ever get to experience.

Then it hit me. *My life would never be the same again.* This beautiful child would not sleep placidly in my arms forever. Soon—very soon—he would awaken with a shrill cry for love, food, and a dry diaper.

As my friend Lynn Miller has humorously observed, that's also the same way we leave the world in our old age. Those cries for attention and personal needs would only get louder and more frequent in the days and months ahead. He would get runny noses, diaper rash, and for kicks, throw up now and then. His sleep patterns would change without warning, which meant my wife's and my sleep patterns (but mostly hers) would be altered too. Our home decor would quickly become twenty-first-century Fisher Price. Our conversations with friends and family— and each other—would concentrate on him. Our disappearing social calendar would be dictated by his schedule.

The family budget would absorb dozens of new line items directly related to his care (word of advice to new parents: you never budget enough for diapers). Nearly every waking thought would include him in some way. In truth, he had become the center of our universe and would instantly become the driving force of our home life.

On the surface, that seems perfectly normal. It's almost instinctive. It only takes holding your newborn for the first time before everything starts revolving around them. They need you. They are helpless. They are cute. They are *yours*.

The One Thing

But should they be the center of your universe? Is that truly what is best for you, them, and your home? The Bible offers us another answer.

According to Scripture, who is the center of the universe?

a. You (remember, I said according to Scripture, not society),
b. Your child(ren),
c. Jesus?

The apostle John tells us that from the very beginning, Jesus was with God and through him all things were made.[9] Later, Paul shares that God's plan is "centered on Christ."[10] The author of Hebrews reminds us that Jesus is the same "yesterday and today and forever."[11]

So if Jesus never changes and is the sole focus of God's plan for humanity—the center of the universe, if you will—then guess what? When your children were born, Jesus *remained* the center of the universe.

God's plan didn't change even though your life did in countless ways. Your child was born into a world where everything came to be because of Jesus. In fact, Jesus himself declares throughout Revelation that he, like God, is not just the *center* of the universe, but the *entire* universe—the Alpha and Omega.[12] He is the One Thing from which every other thing derives.

The movie *City Slickers* remains one of my favorites. In so many ways, I identify with Billy Crystal's tightly wound and sometimes neurotic character, Mitch McDonnell. A businessman in search of something more in life than meetings and office politics, Mitch convinces his two closest friends to accompany him to a Colorado dude ranch for a week away from it all. They will ride horses, breathe in the mountain air, learn to herd cattle, and hopefully rediscover virility to the highest order. Of course, things sure sounded better in the brochure than the reality of their trip. To be honest, I don't think I would have fared much better.

My favorite scene is when Mitch and their crusty ranch

leader, Curly, are riding side-by-side on the open prairie. Curly, masterfully played by the late Jack Pallance, offers Mitch his secret to life. He says to the ever-searching city slicker, "One thing, just one thing. You stick to that, and everything else don't mean nothin'."

Mitch is baffled. Puzzled, he asks Curly for what the one thing is.

"That's what you got to figure out," Curly replies. And so do you.

Curly's philosophy works at a secular level. If money is your one thing, then everything else becomes meaningless. The same goes for status, looks, and popularity. From a Christian perspective though, if Jesus is your one thing, then everything else actually *takes on* significant meaning. Life is enhanced, not diminished. Your children aren't relegated to a secondary consideration. They are lifted up within the rubric of knowing Christ. Putting Jesus first means your kids will be elevated within his love, too.

Your children are not your one thing. Neither is your spouse. They are gifts from the One. Your One Thing is Jesus. This is your starting point for making your house a home.

Don't Make Me Pull This House Over

Reclaiming your home life is not about a Thomas Kincaid winter scene of a family snuggling by the fireplace while the snow and wind whirl wildly outside (although it's not a bad example). Reclaiming your home is all about establishing a safe and accepting place where the love of God can be modeled and taught. The home is God's training center.

The journey of family life begins, ends, and continues with Jesus as the primary focus. It's not about you. It's not about your children. It's about what your children learn about Jesus from you. Max Lucado shares powerful imagery about how our lives are really analogous to the moon.[13] We are simply here to reflect the light of the Son. Without him, we are a cold, dark rock floating through outer space. But when the Son's light hits us, we become a wondrous sight indeed. We become a reflection of Christ to our kids.

That's a tall order—one God takes seriously. And so should we.

According to Barna Research, thirty-seven percent of Americans have children under age eighteen living in their house. Among married couples, almost half have kids. That means a lot of people out there have a lot of responsibility.

So how do you reestablish a home within your house? Let's look at some ideas for you to put into practice.

1. Get to know your kids again. Find out about their favorite music groups. Ask them about what things at school they enjoy *and dislike*. It is important for them to be able to share that math is driving them crazy. That flags an academic area in need of extra attention, and it also provides an emotional release for the child. Solicit their opinions about world events. You might be amazed at what they know (my son recently informed me about a potential new planet that scientists have identified in our solar system, named Sedna—news to me!). Know their friends, not just their names, but also learn about their personalities and interests. Invite them over. Your child lives twenty-four hours per day just as you do. Learn as much as you can about those hours when they are not under your direct care.

2. Eat together. Not to overkill the message, but since we all have to eat, it's the perfect excuse to be together. If you're a chronically on-the-go family, then bring the fast food back to your home to eat at the table together.

How often does your entire family eat a meal together? In biblical times, and even in many modern European cultures, the meal represents much more than feeding time. It is a social occasion for families and friends to share together in conversation. A friend of mine returned from Spain, where he had three-hour dinners each night. Can you imagine any American, especially with kids, spending three hours on dinner? We want to sit down, eat it right away, and move on. In fact, the average mealtime in America is about fifteen minutes.

3. Get together with other homes. You're not alone in your quest for home-ness. Other families are seeking it, too. Through church or school, invite other families into your home. Share past traditions and begin new ones with the help of others.

4. Limit television and technology. How much time do you and your kids spend with technology? The U.S. Census Bureau notes that the ratio of television sets in the home per child is 7:2. That's right—each child has over three to choose from. The average child spends over four hours per day watching the tube. By the time they graduate high school, kids will have spent more time watching television than in the classroom.[14] Add in computer usage with the national averages now showing more than one personal computer per household and Internet usage of several hours per day. You can now see the challenge for families, even when they are under the same roof, is that they still are not together.

Admittedly, as kids grow older, this will change. Teenagers need their space, and technology is a big part of that space. But at the same time, it is not entirely healthy to let them hole up away from the family. They need to come up for air. They need to realize that they remain part of the home.

5. Schedule a family night. It may sound old-fashioned, but most kids love it. Designate a night when everything is off-limits except family. It's really a modern way of practicing the Sabbath.

We tend to get caught up in Old Testament concepts of the Sabbath, but the modern application is to separate yourself and your family from the pull of the culture. Scheduling a special night when you focus just on each other is a wonderful way to honor God's call to separate from the world on a regular basis.

6. Invite God. Remember that God is part of your family, too. It's not all of you *and* him. It's all of you, *including* him. Think of that when planning time together. Chapter 7 will detail this more, but set the guilt monster aside. Many well-intentioned Christian parents struggle in this area. But Deuteronomy 6:7-8 says to tell our kids about God when they get up and go down. They need to see God in everyday life. So even if you can't read or study Scripture every night, be sure to share God's goodness as you're on the go. Talk about nature: rainbows, rainstorms, the like. Talk about feelings: sadness, happiness, frustrations. Talk about others in need. Look and talk about God in every nook and cranny of the world. You will find God is there.

Funeral conversations fascinate me. Talk with the children of an elderly saint gone home. They begin sharing special memories of when they were kids. But these stories don't focus on vacations or gifts or special events. They often return to funny stories of how Mom or Dad's sense of humor would make normal events hilarious. They talk about their quirks. They talk about their passions. They talk about their pitfalls. They talk about life *at home.* That's where real life happens.

Singer Geoff Moore asks in his song *When All is Said and Done,* "Will they say I loved my family?" Interestingly, when we die, the answer to that question has a lot to do with what kind of home we developed, not what kind of house we lived in.

Discussion Questions

1. What kind of home did you grow up in? Were you together regularly?
2. What special memories do you have of your childhood home?
3. How often is your family together under the same roof and doing something *together?* What are ways you can increase that?
4. If you died today, what would your family say about the home you fostered?

EMPOWERING THE PARENT

3

There's a Spouse in the House

Marriage vows are serious stuff. A public declaration by two different people that from now on, *everything* will be shared: The good and bad times. Prosperity and poverty. Sickness and health. Marriage is mutually exclusive and exclusively mutual. "And the two are united into one. . . ."[1]

Marriage is an extraordinary concept. The complexity of bringing together two individuals who have lived their own lives for eighteen or thirty-five years is like a first-time chemistry experiment. Habits have been solidified, opinions formed, and personal preferences set in place. What happens when they combine is unique to each partnership. Of course, love holds it all together—love for God and each other.

There must be something to it though. Insurance statistics show that married people have a much lower mortality rate than single people, especially as we age. Despite all the common jokes, it must be good for the heart.

Marriage is honorable[2] and represents the union between God and his people.[3] It was one of the first institutions in creation. And it came long before Cain. God first. Marriage second. Then, the kids. (See Heaven's Priority from chapter 1.)

Why did you get married?

Hopefully, your answer is something like "Because I love Tom" or "Because I wanted to spend my life with Becky." There are others, to be certain.

And I cannot state strongly enough that Tom, Becky, or whatever your spouse's name may be, is more important than your children.

Say it to yourself right now: (Spouse's name) is more important than (kids' names).

We have to say it to ourselves repeatedly because our culture has told us that (kids' names) are the center of our universe (remember chapter 2). No way. Jesus is the center of the universe. Your kids wouldn't even be here without you and your spouse.

Which Came First?

You cannot be a good parent without first being a good spouse. As Ken Canfield, president of the National Center for Fathering, notes, "When you strengthen (the loving bond you have with your spouse), you provide an atmosphere of security in your home in which your children can grow."[4] A godly, loving marriage is the *foundation* upon which the rest of family life is built. Children need that sturdiness from the onset.

Unfortunately, spouses in too many marriages today no longer see each other as husband and wife. Instead, they have morphed into Mom and Dad—or even worse, "the mother of our children" or "the father of our children." My wife and I made a pledge to each other before our first child was born that we would never directly call each other Mom or Dad in front of our kids. We still today use our first names or a romantic nickname. It is our way of protecting not only the sanctity, but the superiority, of our marriage throughout our life together.

I was a husband before I was a father. I still am today, and I intend to nurture that priority. It makes all the difference.

One of the greatest gifts you can give your kids is to first be spouses. The word "spouse" comes from the Latin word that means "to pledge." You made a promise on your wedding day—*to your spouse*, not your yet-to-arrive kids. That pledge was between you and your mate, and that pledge is what holds everything together in the home.

You know the statistics. Divorce is more common than staying marriages. And though money still reigns as the topic of choice for most arguments, children are still a commonly cited reason for marital strife. As the doctors at the Minirth-Meier Clinic noted, when the first child arrives, a host of new pressures descend upon the marriage:[5]

—increased friction and power struggles
—more opportunity for failure (low self-esteem spouses can now fail as parents, too)
—kids have many more needs than adults, often intense and needing immediate response
—increased financial pressures

I'm not a marriage counselor, but in the face of these inevitable distractions, giving priority to your spouse and being a spouse are vital for keeping your marriage strong and healthy.

Back to the Beginning

What first attracted you to your spouse? The eyes? The laugh? The wit? Something pulled you in, didn't it?

And when the big day arrived, maybe kids were something in the back of your mind, but on the front burner was the man or woman with whom you would share the rest of your life.

When was the last time you and your spouse went out on a date? Took a long weekend? Did anything that bordered on romantic?

How much time each week do you spend talking together? Not about the children, but about your own lives. Your hopes and dreams. Your faith life. Your new interests.

Rekindling the romance may sound like talk-show fare, but it really is essential. As author Bob Moeller says, "It seems to be a natural law—like gravity—that all relationships will decay from a state of health and organization to one of chaos unless there's a stronger contravening force in the marriage."[6] I like that phrase—a "contravening force." Marriage was meant to counter the other forces of the world that vie for your attention and allegiance. Dare I say that marriage, when kids arrive, is intended to stay contavening. It is meant to be self-protective, . . . even against the whirlwind force of now becoming parents.

When is the last time you and your spouse reminisced about how you met, courted, and were married? Relive those original days when it all came together. Better yet, share the memories and images with your children.

If you have a wedding video or photo album, dust it off and look at it again—*together.* Show it to your kids. Sure, you may hear protests of "Boring!" at first, but you will be surprised how many kids are enthralled at seeing *and hearing* about your courtship and marriage. You may find frequent requests to see and hear it again.

The older the kids, the more smart-aleck comments can be expected about hairlines, waistlines, and fashion back then, but it's still a sign they are engaged. Let them rib you.

Tell stories about when you first met. Share them with your kids. Let your kids see you as spouses, too, so they know it's not all about them.

If kids grow up only knowing you as parents, they will miss the best part—knowing how you became parents, which all began with becoming spouses.

Also be sure to share affection openly with your children. I especially encourage husbands and wives to hug and kiss in front of their sons. With so much machismo being thrust upon our sons culturally, they need to know that a "real man" (to use our culture's term) loves his wife with the utmost care and affection—just as Jesus loves the church.[7]

And the *Three* Shall Become One

When my wife and I were planning our wedding ceremony with our pastor, he suggested that he would camp in Ecclesiastes 4:12. I was a brand-new Christian at the time, so the thought of an Old Testament passage being the centerpiece of our wedding felt archaic. Then he read it to us: "Though one may be overpowered, two can defend themselves. A cord of three strands is not quickly broken" (NIV). He could tell by my expression that I still didn't get it.

"Steve," he said, "your commitment is to more than Liz. Your commitment is to Christ. There are three of you getting married." I have never forgotten that. Have you?

A God-centered marriage is a cord of *three* strands. Yes, I adore my wife. But it is my adoration and commitment to Jesus that provides the third strand, making our collective bond unbreakable.

Not only is this scriptural truth essential for couples to embrace through their marriage, it is the greatest gift they can pass along to their children. Imagine what happens if your children see more than just Mom and Dad, but instead, see Mom and Dad *actively* growing and loving the Lord too. They learn that the marriage and the home is not just about them. They also learn that the marriage and the home are not just about Mom and Dad either. It's all about Jesus.

How strong is the third cord—Jesus—in your marriage today? Have you actively pursued his presence in your marriage? If not, take time to talk and pray as a couple about ways to make your partnership centered first on him, and then on you.

Many couples, even in strong marriages, struggle from time to time with their spiritual intimacy. Therapist Scott Stanley and his colleagues recognize that this can be a scary place for couples to go, but once the initial hurdles have been overcome, great blessings await. Here is a list of the things that draw couples closer together in their spiritual lives, based on what they have witnessed in counseling many marriages over the years:[8]

—Sharing their individual spiritual walks: thoughts about God, faith struggles, answered prayer
—Sharing Scripture together: reading and discussing the Bible together, sharing devotional thoughts, simply talking about something God laid on your heart
—Praying together: if this has been a struggle, consider at least discussing prayer concerns and needs
—Worshipping together: attending church together, singing praise hymns, giving thanks (I would add participating in acts of generosity together)
—Sharing ministry: get involved in a structured opportunity through church or a charity, or create your own opportunities to show God's love to others
—Taking communion together: a chance to be side by side during a powerful remembrance of spiritual oneness with Christ and each other

You may ask what this has to do with parenting. I would answer, "Everything." Because it all comes down to what you see as the parent's ultimate responsibility.

The Parenting Paradigm

In many marriages, the kids eventually arrive—what Bill Cosby calls "the most beautifully irrational act that two people in love can commit."[9] And now this foundation of three—you, your spouse, and the Lord—is in place to nurture and raise children.

Here's another multiple-choice question. According to Scripture, what is the main priority of parenting?

> a. Protect your kids,
> b. Make your kids happy,
> c. Point your kids to God?

David urged parents to teach children "to fear the LORD"[10]—to revere, to follow, to worship God with their whole lives. The key is that we are to *teach* them, to lead and demonstrate a godly life, to show the way. Your role is to equip your children based on your marriage's strengths. "A godly father and mother form a parenting team," writes Ken Canfield, "in which they complement each other to the benefit of the children."[11] Put another way: the child looks to you and sees you looking to God, so they look to God as well. The process is that simple, centered on God's center—Jesus.

The problem is that many parents never get this paradigm right. The children become the central focus of the family, and it never changes. Not only does that ascribe too much attention to the kids; it also keeps Jesus from being fully worshipped as the true center of life. The result is kid-centered, not God-centered, families.

Raising your children is one of your highest priorities *and privileges*. God has God-sized expectations for parents and looks to us to follow through on that responsibility. But God also expects us to do so with Jesus at the center of it all.

God-centered families are not centered on the children. God-centered families focus on God becoming the center of the children's lives.

A Word about Grandparents

One final truth about marriage: they don't happen without marriages that went before them. The grandparents. And I believe that grandparents' marriages can also be a positive influence on their grandchildren.

In a workshop one time, a concerned grandfather lamented, "I raised my kids better than that. Now they are doing it to my grandchildren." I asked him to elaborate. Though he lived in the same city as his children, he rarely saw them or his grandchildren. They were never at home, so there was no use in calling.

While he longed for a visit, they were picking up the younger kids from daycare and driving the older kids to soccer practice, band rehearsal, and dance class. Dinner came in McDonald's bags that were delivered to the back seat of the fast-moving minivan. Cell phones blared as parents kept in touch with each other like air traffic controllers making sure that departure and arrival times were synchronized.

I sympathized with him and asked if he had ever told them how he feels. "I have several times," he shared. "Only they tell me, 'Dad, it's different nowadays. You just don't understand.'"

Times *have* changed. God, however, has not.

The role of grandparents in maintaining God's priority

for the family is critical. Grandparents often serve as the family leaders emeritus. They still hold some sway over the current leaders. They rule from experience and wisdom.

"Grandchildren are the crowning glory of aged," says Proverbs 17:6. In many ways, the aged are the crowning glory for their grandchildren. And one of the main reasons is that the grandparents' marriage is (usually) a slower one.

My children, who can be quite finicky about meals, eat double helpings at grandma's house. Why? Likely because they slow down enough to do so. When you're at grandma's, there's no daily agenda. There's no list of places to go. You simply come in and spend the day doing whatever God leads you to do. We'll explore this more in coming chapters.

In another key role, grandparents remind us that all the parental psychobabble today is often more babble than psychology. Dr. Benjamin Spock said this:

> I think that parents ought to get some idea of how the so-called "experts" have changed their advice over the decades, so that they won't take them deadly seriously, and so that if the parent has the strong feeling, "I don't like this advice," the parent won't feel compelled to follow it. . . . So don't worry about trying to do a perfect job. There is no perfect job. There is no one way of raising your children.

Isn't that a great quote? I remember after our son was first born, calling my mom and asking how she ever did it. I'll never forget her reply: "Just love 'em." She, and certainly my grandmothers, never had a 300-page manual on what to expect. They didn't have PhD's and MD's telling them what to do, and the danger of not doing it. They didn't have the latest round of research. All they had were their hearts and the advice of those who had gone before.

If we're honest, parents today have too much

information. No matter how well intentioned the sources, we are told far too much. That's why grandparents offer a great way for everyone—parents and kids—to return to the simple model of "just love 'em."

"Now, more than ever before," says John MacArthur, "is the time for Christians to declare and put on display what the Bible declares: God's standard for marriage and the family is the *only* standard that can produce meaning, happiness, and fulfillment."[12] He's right. The fulfillment we look for in our family lives comes only when they are built upon the solid rock of Jesus and a loving couple—loving each other and loving the Lord. Three strands. Unbroken.

There is a spouse in your house—a spouse before becoming a parent.

Discussion Questions

1. When is the last time you and your spouse had a getaway? When is the last time you looked at your wedding photos and video? Have you shown them to your children?

2. What do you believe about Jesus's role in your marriage? Is he fulfilling that role today? Why or why not?

3. What do you see as your primary role as a parent? To keep kids happy? To keep them safe? To point them to God?

4. How can you incorporate your children's grandparents into their lives?

4

Kids Will Say No When You Do

Kids see the world differently than you and me. They see and hear everything, including everything you do and say. They also emulate much of what they observe. This can be a good or bad thing—*depending on us parents.*

They see and hear you holler at an inconsiderate motorist. Inside, they tell themselves that *that* is how people drive cars. They see you rush out the door on your way to work with no time for breakfast, just a coffee cup in one hand, sloshing to and fro. Over time, they wonder why breakfast should be important to them? They see you working at home, with little time for interruption, and determine that's how it must be in every home. They see your impatience. They hear your irritation. They feel your pain. That's why Harry Chapin's classic hit *Cat's in the Cradle* is such a haunting work. Little boys and girls often *do* grow up to be just like Mom and Dad. And in our culture, that means they will grow up to be hurried, over-burdened, and over-committed adults.

Before we can address how to help your child, we must first look at how you can help yourself. Because like it or not, every day you model for your child a pace of life. At what speed are you living? You also establish a pecking order of unspoken priorities. What is your life telling your children is most important? They are watching. They are listening. They are looking to you for the example.

Are your kids learning Paul's fruits of the spirit in Galatians 5:22-23? Do they regularly see in you joy, patience, gentleness, self-control, and inner peace? Or are they observing the rotten fruit Paul warns about: selfish ambition, arguing, jealousy, envy, and outbursts of anger?

Apples don't fall far from the tree. What kind of apples are you growing?

Hurriedness

Before we start building God-centered homes, we need to start leading God-centered lives. And a God-centered life is an *un*hurried life.

When I researched and wrote my first book, *Time Warped*, I was amazed at the consistency of the Bible's inherent message about God's gift of time: Do less in order to have more of God in your life. *Do less.*

Our culture obviously communicates a different message with a different urgency: Do more and even more . . . and then some more! You aren't enough. You don't have enough. You cannot sit still. You must keep going. Like a car with a jammed accelerator, the speedometer of life keeps jolting forward, faster and faster. My car's speedometer goes up to 160 mph. I am quite certain that the manufacturer never intended for the car to actually operate at such speeds. God made you capable of doing and experiencing much, but I am equally certain that he never intended for you to experience life as a blur.

As sociologist Todd Glitin has observed, "We're a nerve-racked society where people have difficulty sitting back and thinking of the purpose of what they do." Perhaps that is why Rick Warren's *The Purpose-Driven Life* has sold over 22 million copies and was one of the best-selling books of this decade.[1] Everyone knows they are here. But very few know why. Many don't know why because they don't have time to stop and ask themselves the question. They just keep pushing harder on life's accelerator. The result is a perpetually on-the-go life with little, if any, meaningful rest. As physician and author Richard Swenson asserted from his research, the speed of life is the single most important factor affecting personal and social dysfunction.[2] We need to apply brakes, but we can't. For some, they just won't.

In his insightful work *The Life You've Always Wanted*, author John Ortberg makes an important distinction about the constant busyness in our lives. By looking at the life of Christ, Ortberg asserts that Jesus himself was a very busy person. But what separates the Lord's pace of life from yours and mine is that he was never *hurried*. Hurriedness is a disordered heart that breaks our connection to God and holds us back from extending God's love to others when the moment calls.[3]

I believe that Ortberg's insight is critical for combating hurriedness. There is an invisible, but discernible, line that gets crossed when our lives mutate from a state of being busy to the whirlwind of being hurried. Here are just a few personal reflections based on the comments I have heard from years of leading time management workshops:

> —Busy people experience good pressure in order to get something accomplished. Hurried people experience negative stress and churn out their work with lower quality and virtually no personal satisfaction. They just want to get it done and over with.
> —Busy people can still stop and smell the roses, albeit briefly. Hurried people don't even notice the roses are there.

—Busy people experience impatience periodically but can generally tolerate it. Hurried people live in a constant state of intolerable impatience that leads to angry outbursts and deep internal stress. They self-fry from the inside out.
—Busy people get miffed sometimes. Hurried people boil over all the time.
—Busy people still notice the world around them. Hurried people focus only on themselves.
—Busy people still make time for God. Hurried people demand that God make more time for them (which, by the way, is impossible even for God— twenty-four hours is all you get).

The most important question you should ask yourself is: What am I busy doing? Or stated differently: To what is all your hurried activity leading? What is it you are chasing more and more? More money? More status? Or even worse, are you simply stuck in a lifestyle where you no longer know or remember how to slow down? As I have often exhorted parishioners and students, God wants you to have a *fulfilled* life, not a filled one.[4]

A man that I met at a workshop shared one of the most moving stories I have ever heard about making time for his kids. He was the owner of a very successful company whose biggest customer was in the Far East. He traveled there frequently. His family had a big house and every provision they could ever want. But they didn't have him.

One morning, sitting in an airport café eating breakfast, he looked at a photo of his youngest daughter and realized that she was already eight years old. He looked at his bran muffin and couldn't remember the last time he had eaten breakfast with her. He was usually gone by the time she woke up. And when he came home at night, he was too wiped out to even play or help with homework. In that moment, God spoke to his heart as never before. It was a life-changing epiphany. He decided right there that it was time to put his family first, no matter the sacrifice to their finances. The next day he put up his business for sale.

He hasn't missed a breakfast with his daughter since then. He now has the time and energy to be a dad, and he says that decision changed his life forever. Of course it did! He is more patient these days and happier than he can ever remember. He is no longer exhausted at the end of the day. He feels human again. True, we don't all have assets like a corporation to pass along, but we all can reexamine our time commitments to ask what is getting in the way of being a parent, and then get rid of those hurdles.

What makes this topic so critical is that *this* is how your children observe you, too. I often hear hurried people say, "Well, when I walk in the door at home, I'm able to just leave the world behind me." Nice sentiment. Rarely happens though. A cargo train needs over one mile to come to a complete stop. You may slow down when you get home, but what your children need is for you to *stop*. Many parents think slowing down suffices, but a car that has been traveling 80 mph, now traveling 50 mph, is still going too fast to play, hold an attentive conversation, or be spontaneous.

Besides, hurried people's self-assessments are always overestimated. It's been so long since they actually lived an unhurried life that what seems slow to them is still fast within the larger scheme of time and space.

Hurried in the Bible

In Psalm 90:12, a prayer of Moses, it says "Teach us to make the most of our time." Older translations say to "reckon" our time. This implies that there is an accountability between us and God for how we use God's gift of time.

When any gift is invested, we look at the rate of return. What kind of return are you sowing on God's gift of twenty-four hours each day? Or do you squander it? Do you take it for granted?

Martha and Mary were busy preparing the house for Jesus's arrival. However, when he actually showed up, Mary dropped everything to sit at his feet. Martha had a conniption. She beseeched Jesus to tell Mary to start helping her in the kitchen. Instead, Jesus told *Martha* to catch her breath and realize that sitting at his feet was far more important.[5]

What a powerful example this must have been to the people there. But Jesus understood that. He knew that what he did and said in the presence of his followers would serve as a foundation for their future teaching and leading of the church. So it is with you: what you say and do in the presence of your kids serves as a foundation for their future.

As I piggyback on Ortberg's insights, I see several things in Jesus's time management that are woefully missing in our society today—and these are things that our children desperately need to learn *from you*.

1. Others first, me second. Jesus was constantly coming to the aid of an undesirable or rectifying a complex situation. There was no self-promotion in him. No hidden motives. No climbing the corporate ladder. He always had time for someone else. He would give them his undivided attention (there's a phrase we rarely hear anymore).

Even the apostle Paul caught the vision when he wrote, "Don't be selfish; don't live to make a good impression on others. Be humble, thinking of others as better than yourself."[6] *Think of others as better than myself?!* Paul would have made a lousy American. Philanthropy, generosity, and altruism are still alive, but only after *my* needs first have been met.

Not so with Jesus or Paul. Your life matters more to them than their own.

How are you modeling for your children a life that cares about others? It's more than writing a check to charity. How are you reaching out to those in need and making sure your child is participating?

Consider taking them with you on hospital visitations or when delivering a meal to a shut-in. Include them in community and church service projects like raking leaves for the elderly or painting a rundown house. Have them write letters or draw pictures for lonely or sick senior citizens. Pick several toys that have collected dust over the years and donate them to charity. Make sure that part of their allowance is set aside for sharing with others. Sponsor a Compassion child. Instill in them now that God has always been a champion of the underdog, and the way he reaches them today is through us.

2. No formal agenda. Jesus didn't carry a Palm Pilot. He had no day planner. Not even a wristwatch. There was a freedom that allowed Jesus to take in what each day had to offer. Here is where I often hear dissenters argue, "Yes, but Jesus didn't have a fifty-hour per week job like I do. He didn't have a boss or staff or homework to grade. He didn't have to fight freeway traffic or pay a mortgage." No, he didn't. Instead, his job was a 168-hour per week assignment that reported to the Creator of the universe and would ultimately end in his humiliating death as a nobody on behalf of all of us hurried somebodies. So who had the tougher job after all?

I challenge you to schedule one day per week with nothing to do. Leave that one day entirely blank. Call it your Sabbath. Don't accept appointments. Don't attend meetings. Simply leave one day wide open to be spontaneous, to be available, to breathe.

I realize that this sounds good in theory but is difficult in practice. It takes discipline and time to accomplish, so if you know this is just too big of a stretch, start with a half day. Start with one evening per week. But pick a fixed block of time each week and leave it wide open for God, your family, and whatever else might happen. You will be surprised at what will transpire during this time frame and how you'll begin craving it more and more. Why? Because that is how God made you. It is how Jesus lived. Busy, but always accessible.

3. Always making time for God. Jesus did not let the world run away with his ability to connect with God. The Father was his source of life. He constantly went to the source. He urged others to seek this "living water," too.[7] God was always his priority.

Jesus often prayed. He often talked with God. There was nothing more important than tapping into his life source. I wonder if so many people are running on fumes today because they no longer fill themselves with the true power source of life. As physician Christine Sine says, "Since our lives are increasingly disconnected from the rhythms of God's world, we do not hear the underlying whisper of God's heartbeat that is meant to sustain us."[8]

How do you measure up? Are you putting others' needs ahead of your own? Is your life governed by your to-do list and weekly calendar? Is your time with God decreasing while your time with other things is increasing? Do you hear the whisper of God's heartbeat?

What are your answers to these questions saying to

your children? Are they seeing you performing acts of generosity that go above and beyond the call of need (see 2 Corinthians 8)? Are they seeing sacrifices for the welfare of others? Are they seeing a daily schedule that allows for the unexpected and spontaneous? Are they aware of consistent relationships with God? When you get down to it, what better lessons could we teach our kids than to care for others, care for God, and make sure we don't saturate our schedules to the place where those two things can't happen.

Remember what Jesus said are the greatest commandments? Love God and love others. It really is that simple. Unfortunately, the way many adults live would say, "Love self and love stuff" and ask God to bless activities that promote self and stuff. Doesn't quite work that way, does it?

Train a Child

A pivotal verse to ponder is Proverbs 22:6: "Teach your children to choose the right path, and when they are older, they will remain upon it." To help your children choose that path, it helps if you are walking on it, too.

When you survey society, one of the things that becomes clearer is that impatience and hurriedness is coming out in younger and younger kids. They are being enveloped by it from the youngest ages because it is all they have ever seen in adults.

A father of four joked with me one time about how the only night of the week when he and his wife saw each other was Friday. Every other night they were out with the kids at rehearsals and practices. Around 9:00 p.m. each night, their minivans would converge on the garage, and the family would be reunited for a few minutes before bedtime called. He chuckled as if there was nothing he could do about it, but this was no laughing matter. This was an absurd way to live. But in comparison with society, it was actually quote normal.

I believe it's normal because people no longer look for another way. Pamela Evans, author of *The Overcommitted Christian,* calls it an addiction.[9] She's right. *Addiction* comes from the Latin word meaning "to be given over." Many of us have been given over to our time constraints like a prisoner before the warden. We no longer know how to lead a healthy-paced life. What is normal is living at 200 mph.

I believe this is the single biggest misconception in our culture today regarding time. We have accepted a hurried lifestyle as normal because so many others are living at the same pace. We attribute a sense of comfort with its prevalence. There is also a prevalence of cancer in our society, and I know no one comfortable with that. The danger with normalizing hurriedness is that we no longer look for an antidote.

Recently, my two young sons and I were at the local lawn and garden shop, which also doubles as a pet store. My boys love going there to see guinea pigs, turtles, snakes, fish, birds, lizards—just about any animal that fits in an aquarium case. In the center of it all is a tall wooden post where an enormous multicolored parrot perches. He belongs to the store owner and has been there for as long as I can remember. He never bothers the customers. He sits like a feathered sentry, watching the comings and goings of the small retail shop.

This particular day, my oldest son was intrigued with the tiny brown gerbils that scurried around one of the aquarium tanks. Two gerbils had jumped onto a wire wheel and began running as fast as their tiny pink feet would go. The wheel was moving so fast that occasionally one of them would fall off, and then jump back on as if nothing ever happened.

My son was delighted at their antics, but also a bit bewildered. "Daddy?" he asked. "Why do the gerbils keep running so fast?"

Before I answered, I was struck that we are not much different from the gerbils. It is as if we have jumped onto our individual gerbil wheels and started running faster and faster. We glance over and see other gerbils running equally fast, some even faster. So we run faster still. Now we're moving!

But then I caught a glimpse of the gorgeous parrot, stretching his wings and also watching the gerbils. In my mind, a Doolittle-ish dialogue began as I could almost hear the parrot answer my son for me and for everyone on their wheels: *They run so fast because they have forgotten they are in a cage.*

Are you in a cage, too? Be brutally honest with yourself. Do you feel trapped by your commitments? When is the last time you felt free to be yourself and be spontaneous? What drives your daily activities?

Saying No to Say Yes

For many of you, reclaiming the throne of your home that Junior has happily climbed into means developing a lifestyle that allows you time to sit on your chair. One of the reasons many parents have abdicated leadership is because they no longer have time. Make the time by doing *less*. As Moses said, make the most of the time.

Now is the time to start taking steps at slowing down your runaway lifestyle. There is never a better day to start. I encourage you to read and go through the personal exercises in my book *Time Warped*. Seek out other biblical time stewardship resources (Richard Swenson's *Margin: The*

Overload Syndrome is excellent). Meet with your pastor or a close friend and confess your hurriedness. But whatever you do, realize that you need to slow down not just for yourself, but also for your children's sake.

The earlier mentioned proverb says that we are to train children in the way they should go. The challenge is that children don't know the way. We can lead them down a dark alley where the world races by in an impersonal and scary blur. Or we can lead them down a wide path into the open fields of God.

They are watching the path you travel because that is the path they will travel, too: that same proverb reminds us that when they are older, they will *not* depart from the path. If you want them to grow up and live a more stable and balanced life than you, then help them by helping yourself. You slow down first.

Discussion Questions

1. Revisit the fruits of the spirit in Galations 5:22-23. How many of these do you experience on a regular basis? How can you experience them more frequently?

2. Look back at the last two weeks. What have your experiences been with your children? What have your kids witnessed? What have they learned about the world?

3. Have you ever sat down and talked with your children about the importance of slowing down and resting in God? If not, what would you tell them?

4. Why are you so hurried these days? Read Luke 10:38-42. Are you more like Mary or Martha? Why did Jesus say that Mary had found the better thing?

DETHRONING THE CHILD

5
Nobody's Home

Nearly everyone has a Little League story. Maybe yours is a soccer story or a play rehearsal story. But nearly everyone has a story about how an extra-home activity went terribly awry . . . because of the parents.

Recently, a Pennsylvania father was arrested as coach of a T-ball team. He paid $25 to a boy on the team to throw a baseball into the groin of a disabled teammate so he couldn't play in an upcoming game.[1] League rules required each child to play three innings, but according to the national press report, this man's daughters were on the team, and he didn't want to lose. It's almost beyond comprehension. Correction: It *is* beyond comprehension.

A youth hockey dad *fatally* strikes another dad because their kids got into a tussle on the ice during practice. He's now serving a prison term for manslaughter.[2] Stand-clearing brawls at high school sporting events between *parents* and fans. I've even heard of near fisticuffs following band competitions. Sports journalist, Seth Davis, recently commented on how awful basketball dads have become in his experience covering the game.[3] Shouldn't the *children* be the ones making headlines?

Fortunately, most of our stories don't end in jail time or injury. But if Jesus's warning in Matthew 5:22 about calling a brother "*Rhaka*" (idiot) holds, many of us would be guilty as charged.

To be fair, renegade parents are the exception, but they also have a way of ruining the experience for everyone. I vividly remember attending my nephew's baseball game one summer night. Several rows behind me, the father of one of his teammates, who was pitching, kept barking out orders like a drill sergeant: "Follow through!" "Hit the corners!" "Focus!"

And, of course, when the umpire called any pitch a ball, the father lit up the night with a string of jaunts and verbal attacks. Inning after inning it continued. He wouldn't shut up. By the fourth inning, nearly every other parent there wanted to grab their kid and go home, or at least go sit in their car with the stereo blasting. He had ruined it for everyone. But worst of all, he had ruined it for his son.

Every time the kids left the field for the dugout, you could read his son's body language. Shoulders sagging. No eye contact. Painful embarrassment since no other parents were making themselves into buffoons. The poor kid just wanted to crawl underneath the bench.

Again, this example is still the exception, but it is becoming more and more common all the time. According to one Little League administrator who oversees a positive parenting alliance, "Before it was coaches helping the kids who were having trouble controlling their emotions. Now it is, 'Let's provide leadership to help the coaches control the parents.'"[4]

Considering that seventy percent of children quit playing sports by age twelve,[5] it begs the question of what kind of impact extra-home activities are having on our homes.

Extra-home? The common term, of course, is extracurricular, which implies something done outside normal school or work hours. But in truth, nearly all extracurricular activities happen outside the home, and that has big implications for our discussion. Thus, *extra-home* is the term I'll use.

We have a lot to choose from. There are one-hundred-eighty thousand Little League teams with two and one-half million players and over one million volunteers worldwide. On any given night in the summer, there are ten thousand Little League games going on somewhere on the planet.[6] Soccer has baseball beat. There are over three million players in the U.S. Youth Soccer programs with over a half million volunteers.[7] There are fifty-two thousand Boy Scout troops with nearly one million scouts and over a half million volunteers.[8] There are Girl Scouts. Bands. Drama troops. Swim teams. Chess clubs. None is better than another. None is worse than another. The point is that families are not at home.

Why We Do What We Do

The challenge of extra-home activities is tricky. There is no question that some kids thrive in extra-home activities and take home powerful lessons about teamwork, hard work, and dedication that will benefit them for a lifetime. Absolutely. I'm one of them. So are other better-known names like Senator Bill Bradley (all-American college and pro basketball player) or Supreme Court Justice Sandra Day O'Conner (former Girl Scout). The impact of music, drama, and art is equally impressive.

But there is also no question that many kids today are involved in too many extra-home activities, or even worse, are involved in activities even though they don't want to be.

The first question we must unpack is, Why are your kids in extra-home activities? There are only two possible answers: They asked to be in them, or you made them be in them.

Now it's true that many kids' first reaction to anything new is, "Naah, I'd rather not." They are immature and uncertain. So an initial coaxing is certainly appropriate.

"C'mon, just give it a try. You might like it." Parents need to encourage expanded boundaries. But what if the child is more adamant? There is a line that every family has to define where participation in extra-home activities becomes coercive, not voluntary.

Beyond this, there is the question about whether or not the child even likes the activity. You might be surprised.

Let me share a story that every parent needs to hear. Tonya (name changed), who attended one of my workshops, was a mother of three active children, ages three to ten. During a group discussion, she raised her hand and asked if she could share her story. She not only shared it; she also changed some lives in that room.

Her middle child, Travis, then an eight-year-old, was a soccer fanatic, according to Tonya. He played all the time and was quite good. Soccer shirts, shorts, and shoes cluttered his bedroom. Soccer balls dotted the backyard near a giant practice goal. Game schedules hung on the refrigerator door. This was Soccer Central.

That spring, when sign-ups for the summer league began, Tonya was certain that her husband was handling Travis's registration. He was certain that Tonya was taking care of it. Neither of them did. The deadline for registering passed, and their soccer fanatic was left off a roster. They begged club organizers to make a special exception. Their family had been mainstays of the league. But community demand was so high that nothing could be done. They were out of luck. No soccer that summer.

The emotional wringing Tonya and her husband went through was intense. They were upset with each other. They were upset with the league. They were upset with life itself. How would they ever break the news to Travis? How could they have been so stupid? The summer was surely ruined, they fretted. Three months of a grumpy eight-year-old daydreaming about the soccer field all because Mom and Dad couldn't get their act together for a five-minute sign-up.

Finally, one night soon after their blunder, Tonya and her husband mustered up the gumption to sit down with Travis and break the bad news. They had rehearsed their explanation, even role-playing it several times. They sat on his bed and lit the fuse. When they had finished, they braced themselves for the inevitable backlash. Instead, there was a strange silence, and then Travis calmly spoke up. "That's okay," he said, " I'd rather stay at home with you this summer."

They were flabbergasted, to say the least. The ranting, the raving, the contortions, the convulsions, the accusations . . . ? None came from Travis. Instead, an understanding third grader shared that he was quite content being at home that summer. Some fanatic, huh?

She went on in tears to tell the workshop attendees of how that summer would become the best summer they ever had as a family. Instead of constantly traveling to practices and games, they were together *at home*, and they grew closer than ever before. It changed their lives profoundly, even to this day.

Tonya said the greatest lesson in all of this was to make sure that you are asking your children if they like their extra-home activities. She was sure her son was a soccer fanatic. Turns out he could take it or leave it. And when given the option of being homebound, he gladly took that chance to be *with* his family, not *with his family in the stands*.

Tonya's story is a powerful reminder that sitting on bleachers and watching your child is not parenting. It's being a chauffeur and a spectator. Parenting is active. Spectatorship is passive.

Now, to avoid any misunderstanding, I strongly support you being at your child's games and concerts. Absolutely. Your support in presence alone sends a wonderful message to your kids. But before you make the commitment as a home to participate in extra-home activities, here are a few guidelines to consider first.

1. Practice, practice, practice. The child has been asked and answered that they love both *practice* and the games. Notice the emphasis on practice. Most kids enjoy games and the pomp of being out on the field or court. But do they like getting up early for practice? Do they mind the hot, humid temperatures? Do they feel pinched socially? The legend of Larry Bird as a high school basketball star was not centered around his prolific scoring and rebounding. The legend grew from how many hours per day he would practice. If your kids look forward to practicing as much as the performance, you probably have stumbled upon a real interest or passion. If they constantly complain about practices or it takes a crane to get them there, you may want to reconsider.

2. It's not about you. A second guideline is making sure that *you* have no vested interest in the activity. We all publicly deny the possibility that our children's participation and performance in extra-home activities is a reflection on us personally, but there are droves of parents who are vicariously building or tearing down their own self-worth based on whether or not Junior is a first chair violinist or hit the game-winning shot. If your child quit an extra-home activity today, would you be okay with that? This is a tough question for parents to answer.

We look out on the horse stable and see our daughter riding with a big smile on her face. She seems happy, and that makes us happy. But what if she plopped down in the backseat tonight after her ride and said, "I'm done riding. I'd rather do something else." How would you react? Certainly more probing is needed, but would you insist they continue? "I paid good money for this." "You don't ever give up in this family." Those kinds of responses are clear indicators that the extra-home activity is about you, not them. What you feel as an adult is irrelevant to the situation. It really is.

3. Coming of age. A third guideline is that the participating child is not under age five or six. Three-year-old T-ball and soccer leagues have never been God's design. They have human prints all over them. We have Tiger Woods to thank for that (though not his fault directly).

A two-year-old Eldrick Woods walked onto *The Mike Douglas Show* stage one night and putted against legendary comic Bob Hope. Three years later, at age five, he was featured in *Golf Digest* magazine. Nowadays, it's not unusual for children with unique talents to appear on Letterman or Leno. Nor is it unusual for the national press to pick up on stories of potential prodigies. But what makes Tiger's story so compelling—and influential—is that he grew up to become exactly what he predicted: one of the greatest golfers of all time, on track to break all of Jack Nicklaus's records.

As a result, parents across the world have since established the standard that the sooner Junior starts, the better he or she will become at something. Piano keyboards for my toddler. A hockey stick in my two-year-old's hand. Parents are lining up their kids for extra-home activities before they can even attend preschool. What does that say about us? What does that say to our kids?

Dr. David Elkind, who sounded the alarm twenty years

ago in his groundbreaking work, *The Hurried Child,* sums it up well in a more recent book, *Ties That Stress:* "The shift from the perception of the child as innocent to the perception of the child as competent has greatly increased demands on maturity."[9] And God has a design for maturity that he never intended for us to speed up, especially for our littlest children. Plus, Elkind says, there is no reliable evidence that starting children early in sports gives them an advantage or edge.[10]

Carla was a stay-at-home mom of two young daughters. Her husband, Tim, and she had signed up their oldest, Kami, for a community T-ball league for three-year-olds. They were so excited to get Kami involved with other kids.

Tim would come home from work and practice tossing the ball to Kami in the front yard. Occasionally, she would get a finger on the ball, but usually it sailed over her shoulder. Tim urged her to catch the ball, but watching the ball roll into the flower beds was quite amusing. Batting was nearly impossible. The spindly Kami could barely lift the bat. Tim showed her how to swing around her waist, but the weight of the bat made her practice swings look like she was golfing. *How will this ever work?* he wondered.

At the first game, all the parents were abuzz. There were cameras flashing and recording. Laughter and exhortations. The miniature players were going through practice drills, doing their best to fit into the spectacle.

Midway through the first inning, Carla had an epiphany. "I sat there looking around and realized we were there for ourselves, not the kids. It was all about us parents oohing and aahing at how cute our kids looked in batting helmets and uniforms. We screamed like crazy when anyone on our team made contact with the ball (which was maybe one out of every three kids). The coaches meant well, but explaining baseball rules to a toddler is like explaining physics to me. They didn't know where to run or why they had to stop at a base and wait. The only thing the kids cared about was the ice cream promised afterward. I mentally stepped back and asked myself, 'What in the world are we teaching Kami? That this is life? This is a family? Running all over town? Having a ball thrown to her every night in the yard?' We were there because all our friends were there. We were there because it meant more to us. We stopped going the next week. Kami never even asked about it again."

Carla's story is important on many levels. But when you consider physical and emotional development in children, organized sports at age three gives *pre*mature a whole new meaning. Carla is right. It is about the parents.

In some cases, there may be a disturbing reverse psychology at play: If we can get Junior overcommitted, suddenly *our* overcommittedness doesn't seem so unhealthy. In other words, if I can get everyone in my life, including my toddler, living at my pace, then everything feels normal. Ever watch three-year-olds playing T-ball? It's not normal. Not even close.

We tell ourselves it's "good for them," but in reality, it's good for us, who feel so much guilt and uneasiness inside from our own hurriedness that we'd rather take the kids down with us too.

I think every parent who signs up their children for any extra-home activity should be required to read Elkind's *The Hurried Child*. What he warned of in the 1980s has only become worse in the present generation of parents.

Peer Pressure

Peer pressure was supposed to stop after high school, right? We finally could live without worry about what others think about our looks, our grades, and our friends. Think again.

Peer pressure among adult parents is overwhelming. "It's not about parents who are over the top," says psychiatrist and author, Alvin Rosenfeld, "It's about a cultural pressure that's endemic."[11] Parents have been sucked into a vortex. The cultural message is that good parents keep their kids active. Active doing what though? In the end, that might be the true measure of success.

I remember a conversation with a woman in our church several summers ago. My oldest son, then five, was not interested in sports of any type. She came up and asked me what his plans were for the summer. "I'm not sure," I replied.

"Little League?" she probed. "No," I said.

"Soccer?" Her voice rising a bit. "No."

She swallowed hard and then exclaimed (she really did shout), "What on earth is he going to do then?!" I smiled and said, "Be a kid."

The subconscious angst in her question really was about her, not my son. She really was asking, "How can you say no to all the peer pressure around us?" I felt sorry for her. Her kids were signed up for everything that moved that summer. And *she* did the signing up. Her summer was about her as a mother, so that when her friends asked her the same question she asked me, she would be ready with a cacophony of clubs, activities, and special events that proved what a great parent she was.

Isn't it true? Don't parents wear as a badge of honor how busy they are in the summer? It's a form of boasting to say that Junior is in this and that and this and that, and that the family is going here and there and everywhere. We cry out for peer approval. "See? Aren't we good parents? We're doing so much for our child." *What* you are doing is yet to be determined.

And isn't it interesting that other parents never ask *children* what they are doing. They ask other parents. That speaks for itself.

David Elkind says, "We don't want our children to feel different from the other children or feel excluded."[12] *We* don't want them to. Yet God made each child different to glorify him. Perhaps we are missing the bull's eye.

You have three responsibilities in your parenting role: God, your spouse, and your kids. That's it. The neighbors, your in-laws, and your church friends are not part of the equation. They are part of your life, to be certain. But you are not here to please them or meet their expectations.

The Inherent Message

The message of extra-home activities has changed over time. It used to be about pursuing activities and areas of interest to a child that weren't offered during school hours. But the message today is much more blunt and insidious. The message is that school is not enough. Home is not enough. Your friends are not enough. You need more. Without it, you're nothing.

Hear my spirit. Sports, music, drama, art, and writing are all very healthy, productive activities for children to experience . . . *with appropriate limits*. But isn't there more to life? "When parents push," say Michael and Diane Medved, "they teach kids to define success in terms of a good school, prestigious job, and earning a lot of money, rather than in terms of spirituality or mastering virtues such as charity, honesty, and reliability."[13]

Somewhere along the line our culture fed us a lie: If

Junior is not enrolled in umpteen different activities, he or she won't be well-rounded. Our kids became living résumés and college applications. And admittedly, schools haven't helped. Extracurriculars mean something to colleges. Nevertheless, a recent Harvard admissions office report described arriving students as decidedly not well-rounded and burnt out before they enter college.[14] The résumé is long and impressive, but the depth of the kid was stunted long ago.

Here's the rub: new research is showing that we've just raised a generation of overcommitted kids. The new findings show that what is best for a child is to find one thing they enjoy doing and do that. They don't have to be all-state at it. They just need to enjoy it.

Setting limits is critical. And often, it's not just limitations on involvement. Many activities today require multiple evening and even weekend commitments. Pastors of all denominational stripes have reported the increased number of family absences on Sundays due to club and school conflicts. Imagine telling God: No time for you today. I've got a gymnastics meet. But that's what we tell God Sunday after Sunday.

Is that being too legalistic? Perhaps. But God does not play second fiddle. As parents, we have to ask ourselves what is more important?

I had a friend whose son played soccer. They had regular Sunday travel games that precluded them from attending worship. My friend told the coach that his son could play all the games Monday through Saturday, but not Sunday. What do you think the coach's response was? "Then he doesn't play at all."

These are tough, tough decisions, but think about it this way. We go out of our way to make sure the kids are at practice. Yet, skipping church is an afterthought. Which preparation do you think will have a bigger impact on their lives in the long run?

Receiving Rest

Jesus said, "Come to me, all of you who are weary and carry heavy burdens, and I will give you rest."[15] Whether you are weary from being a twenty-four-hour shuttle service to and from practices and performances, or whether you carry the heavy burden of parental peer pressure or are desperately wanting to feel good about yourself through your child's participation, Jesus's invitation still stands.

And he wants to give you *and your children* the one thing our culture woefully lacks: rest. Not sleep. Not vegging out in front of a late-night movie. Jesus is speaking of the peace and balance that can fill your heart and your life when you *come to him.*

Notice that he is not going to tap you on the shoulder or call you on the phone to tell you what you already know. He is going to send you an open invitation and wait for you to approach him. And when you do, he has a precious, precious gift to give you.

It's not found at the soccer complex. It's not found in the orchestral pit. It's not found in the scout tent.

He has no problem if you occasionally visit the soccer complex, orchestral pit, and scout tent. He will also be there with you. He is simply opening a door for parents who have signed up their kids for all three at one time. For the time will come sooner rather than later when you need to walk through that door and take in, perhaps for the first time, the fullness of knowing that God couldn't love you anymore than he does right now—no matter how much or what you do (see Romans 8:39).

And by the way, the greatest basketball player of the

modern era, Michael Jordan, started playing basketball as a *sophomore in high school*. Take that, Tiger.

Discussion Questions

1. Why are extra-home activities important to *you?* (Don't answer from your kids' perspectives. Answer from your own heart.)
2. Have you ever worried or felt like your kids were doing too much? That your extra-home activity was putting too much pressure on your home? How did you respond?
3. What is your honest appraisal of your own battle with parental peer pressure? Are there certain couples you are trying to keep up with? Have you ever felt embarrassed when telling another family that your family isn't as busy as theirs? Why do you feel that way?
4. Have extra-home activities impinged upon your churchgoing experience as a family? Where would Jesus be on Sunday morning?

6
Send in the Clouds

What are your memories of childhood? Think about when you were five. What events do you recall? Christmases? Birthday parties? Vacations? What did you do during the summer? Riding bikes? Swimming? Who did you spend time with? Neighbors? Cousins? Yourself?

Remember the game of gazing at clouds and imagining what they were shaped like? I used to sit in my backyard and watch the clouds roll by, seeing faces and animals usually. Sometimes I saw knights with swords brandished, and occasionally I'd see angels. What matters is not what I saw, but that I actually had time to play the game in the first place.

I recently asked a group of kindergartners if they had ever played this game. No hands were raised. Several of them had never even heard of the game.

A basic question needs to be answered. Really it needs to be asked because I think we have forgotten about it. What does it mean to be a kid? What is childhood really all about? What are God's expectations for childhood?

We've already examined how our own hectic lives and extra-home activities can too quickly usher children into adult schedules and activities. So how do we help kids be kids again? When a group of kindergartners have never watched the clouds roll by, red flags rise. Here are the three that rose for me in response to their nonresponse.

Bored in Boise

Several kindergartners told me that watching clouds sounded boring. Nowadays, what doesn't?

Many parents have bought into the common thinking that boredom is bad and its converse, constant activity, is good. Challenge yourself to think about this in a different way. What if boredom is good and constant activity is not?

Boredom can lead to mischief. Boredom can also lead to imagination. It's one of the reasons why video games have been so widely criticized. They combat boredom, but they stifle creativity.

Psychiatrist Alvin A. Rosenfeld, coauthor of *The Over-Scheduled Child,* says, "Given an opportunity to get a little bored, children develop a world of their own. And that's the world that enriches them and society for the rest of their lives."[1]

Imagination feeds on time. Without time, imagination withers. Not scheduled time, but free time. Children can't be told to be creative. You cannot schedule for imagination at 6:00-7:00 p.m. Kids need to be spontaneous and respond to it. Boredom helps to agitate that process.

"If Einstein's parents were alive today, poor little Albert would get a comprehensive evaluation and end up on Ritalin," Rosenfeld says. "Deprived of his daydreams, he might not discover the theory of relativity, but he certainly would focus more fully on the complex demands of fourth-grade math."

In earlier generations, kids used to tell each other, "We're bored." Then they would combine their creative energies to come up with new games and activities. I've talked with many people who have wonderful memories of childhood games using leftover boxes, two-by-fours, a kickball, and other miscellaneous items. Sometimes those ideas were mischievous or misguided, but they were driven by hands-on ingenuity and a child's imagination.

Today's generation gripes to their parents, "We're bored," as if the parents are responsible for changing the boredom. Why? Because their imagination has been so stifled that they don't know what to do. Juniors sit on the throne and demand that Mom and Dad dance before them. Be entertainers. Be their imagination for them.

Stay-at-home parents often lament about having to figure out what to do for their children. One of the best things may be letting them stay bored for a while. You will be surprised what that triggers: a dormant imagination comes to life.

Digital Dependence

Another reason that the cloud game failed with the kindergartners is because it lacks technology. We tend to forget that our youngest generation has grown up surrounded by technology. Toddlers know how to run VCRs. Computer skills are taught as soon as school begins. Our kids know technology inside and out. It seems strange to do anything that doesn't beep or have a remote control.

It's one of the reasons that nature is such an important counter-agent. Not just camping, but simply getting out in the woods or visiting a zoo. We see God's creation, not human creation.

We want our children to be computer literate. But we want them to be cognizant of the world, too.

Be careful of recent marketing tactics in this arena. There is a concentrated effort underfoot in the cellular phone industry to market to children. Early in 2005, Disney announced a partnership with Sprint to market cell phones to eight- to twelve-year-olds.[2] The last thing children need is more technology.

The American Academy of Pediatrics even recommends that children under two not be exposed to screen media at all, and that older kids have no more than one to two hours a day—but not at mealtime and only after kids have played outside, read, or spent some active time.[3] Technology time should be the *least* amount of time kids are spending in comparison to all their other options.

Out of Time

The third reason children may not be looking at clouds is that we are not giving them the time to be kids. Children need time to watch clouds. There may be no more-important statement in this book. They need space, they need freedom, they need the flexibility to be goofy and creative. What they don't need is a bigger pile of adult expectations and schedules.

Here is the great thing about young children: They have no concept of time. To a toddler, thirty minutes is thirty hours. We cannot rob them of this right. We simply have to keep that energy flowing. As Dr. Benjamin Spock once said, "The child supplies the power, but the parents have to do the steering." And the best place for this to happen is with uninterrupted play.

A national survey by the University of Michigan's Survey Research Center found that over the last twenty years, children have lost twelve hours per week in free time, including a twenty-five percent drop in play and fifty percent drop in unstructured outdoor activities. Harvard pediatrician T. Berry Brazelton declares that "play is the most powerful way a child explores the world and learns about himself."[4]

What if our kids were left to be kids? Ida Collier from the Center for Effective Parenting at Arkansas Children's Hospitals says, "Children need physical activity, but that doesn't mean they have to be involved in organized sports. Outside play in a child's neighborhood or a nearby park can fill that just as well."[5]

Once I baked a cake for my wife. Once. I read the instructions on the box and followed them to a tee. The only drawback was that we were out of eggs. Not being a big fan of eggs myself, I said, "Who needs them? The cake will be better without them." So I continued stirring the batter and preheating the oven.

The cake smelled wonderful, with chocolate odors wafting throughout the house. When the timer sounded and I pulled the pan from the oven, it looked perfect. The color of brown was ideal, and its shape was terrific. I was a step away from chefdom.

A few hours later, I went to cut the cake. As my knife entered the top, the entire cake imploded. It all fell into the center because the center was hollow. There was nothing there. Apparently, eggs play a role in keeping everything together. I now had a big chocolate mess on my hands.

Kids are no different. God's recipe is that you give them space and time. Don't hold back. Don't skimp on their experience as a kid.

The single greatest gift you can give your child is the space and time to be a child. You wouldn't take a cake out of the oven after five minutes of baking. You wouldn't remove wet blue jeans from the dryer five minutes into the cycle. So don't take your kids out of their God-given and God-intended space to be a kid.

Child development expert Penelope Leach reminds us, "Many parents find it hard to accept that the best a child can have is every possible, peaceful opportunity for optimal personal development." Notice that she didn't say *performance,* but *development.* Leach continues, "Too many Western parents emphasiz[e] what babies can *do* rather than glorying in the people they are becoming."[6]

What about you? Are you more committed to who your kids are becoming, or are you more concerned about what they are able to do? There is a big difference. Therapist Abraham Schmitt says that "teach(ing) children to perform for themselves and not their parents" is one of the most delicate parent skills to be honed.[7]

Stay-at-Home Families

We have coined a term in our modern culture: the "stay-at-home" mom and dad. What if there were to be "stay-at-home" families. Can you imagine?

A growing underground of families in our culture are becoming stay-at-home families. They are not agoraphobic with a fear of open spaces—far from it. But they have elevated the family's togetherness over individual pursuits.

If you are one of those families, be willing to lovingly challenge other families to consider this option.

Author Marie Sherlock offers a long list of ideas for stay-at-home families in her book, *Living Simply with Children*:[8]

—Board and card games
—Parties and celebrations (not just birthdays either)
—Telling jokes
—Storytelling (your kids should share their stories too)
—Music and dance
—Painting and sculpture
—Volunteer opportunities
—Picnics
—Flying kites
—Treasure hunts
—Projects like building a birdhouse
—Reading to each other
—Playing catch
—Include them in cooking, gardening, and maintenance

If after reading that list, you still feel a bit uneasy about the prospects, ask yourself why. Does the thought of being at home feel awkward? Do you sense peer pressure from neighbors and friends? Have you forgotten how to be at home?

It could be that some parents need to remember what being a kid is all about by opening the door to their own inner child. Re-read the list above. How many of those activities actually sound fun to you as an adult? Most of them, I suspect. Of course. Even though we age and (hopefully) mature, there remains a place in our heart to still enjoy kid-like activities. Be willing to set free the kid in you too. Your kids will sense the change right away.

Caring for Your Gift

Psalm 127:3 says that children are a gift from the Lord. They are a reward.

Let that soak in. Children are a *gift*.

Imagine your best friend gave you an expensive luxury car. It came with all the latest gizmos and upgrades. The car had only ten miles on the odometer. It was one of a kind.

Soon after receiving it, though, you began driving it in the field behind your house. You ran it over hills and through mud bogs. You bounced over branches and ran over small shrubs. The paint was scratched by hundreds of twigs and thorns. The shocks were nearly worn out. The tires were terribly out of balance. And a funny sound came from the exhaust. A few small dents adorned the hood.

The car still looked like a car. It still ran from point A to point B. But it was no longer the luxury car you started with.

One day your friend came over to visit.

How would you react? Would you throw a tarp over

it? Would you lie and say that you got in an accident? Would you be defiant: "Hey, it's my car now, so if I want to rough it up, it's my prerogative."

The problem is that God knows the truth about how we have cared for his gift of our children. Next to Jesus, they are the most precious gift God will ever give us. How are you caring for them? Are they living life as kids? Are they being given time and space to *be* kids? Or have your kids been ridden hard? Have they been overextended? Have they been roughed up by your runaway lifestyle and expectations? Would God recognize them as the children he intended them to be?

Take a hard look at your home tonight. Take a harder look at your kids. And then, tomorrow, take a break and look at some clouds.

Discussion Questions

1. What are your fondest memories of childhood?
2. Can you think of a time when your children were being silly and you made them stop? How can you foster a more free-thinking environment in your home?
3. What are activities that your children enjoy doing with you?
4. What grade would you get if God gave you a report card on allowing your child to be a child? Why do you think that?

ENTHRONING GOD

7

The House of God

Let's say Jesus knocked on your door tonight. Naturally, you let him come inside. What would he see? What would he hear? What would he find and observe under your roof? It may sound far-fetched, but looking upon your home through the eyes of Christ can make a big difference.

If Jesus sat at your dining room table, what would you serve him? If you had some yard work to finish, would you ask him to help? If your cell phone rang in the middle of talking with him, would you answer it? How would your family dynamic change if Jesus took up residence in your home?

I suspect that our priority list would be turned upside down. The TV would be turned off. Mundane chores would be postponed. The evening snooze in the La-Z-Boy would be skipped. We would be like Mary, sitting at Jesus's feet and discovering "the better thing."[1] I envision lively conversation. Maybe a few games. A good snack. And before eyelids grew too heavy, there would be some quality time with the Father.

Getting Your Rest

Scripture actually suggests that day *begins* at night, not at sunrise. In Genesis 1:5 (NIV) we learn that "there was evening, and there was morning—the first day." Hosting Jesus in our homes would create a new nighttime dynamic that would focus on preparing for a new day rather than calling it quits on the day gone-by. The Jews celebrated the Sabbath at sun*down* for this reason.

What is telling about this perspective is that it honors sleep. We have defined a day in terms of when we are awake. We exclude sleeping from the equation. But sleep is a gift from God, to be shared and experienced like all of his other gifts. Why shouldn't it be included in a God-centered home?

Considering that seven in ten Americans suffer from frequent sleep problems, including forty million people with chronic disorders, it seems a solid starting point for building a house of God would be making sure our families are getting enough rest. Even sixty-nine percent of children experience multiple sleep problems during the week.[2] It's hard to grow close to anyone, let alone God, when we're blurry eyed and fuzzy minded.

What would happen if your day began with dinner each evening? You could start seeking God's guidance and participation in your upcoming plans *before they even get started*. Knowing that you have connected with God before the morning sun rises may help you sleep easier too. We awaken not to *start* a new day but to "merge" with God on what he has already been working on.[3] We become God's partner, not a petitioner.

Ensure that your children are getting enough sleep. The house of God includes and acknowledges the importance of physical rest.

Overturning the Tables

Though Jesus never had a permanent home here on earth, there was a house that deeply mattered to him—the Jewish temple. Upon arriving in Jerusalem during his final week of life, the first place he went was the temple. What he found there greatly disturbed him. Merchants and money changers had overtaken the temple. It had become a place of commerce, not worship.

So angered by the scene, Jesus began overturning the tables and chasing away the vendors. He shouted, "You have made it (God's house of prayer) a den of thieves."[4] Obviously, keeping God front and center in the temple was paramount to Jesus. So it is with your house too.

What has taken over your home? Who are the merchants who have set up shop? Nintendo? Microsoft? Homework? Little League? Girl Scouts?

It may be a stretch theologically, but Jesus's ultimate concern was not that business was taking place inside the temple (although I'm sure he would have preferred somewhere else). What upset him so much was that the opportunity for prayer and worship—what the temple was built for—was being snuffed out. Those who truly longed to connect with God were unable to do so.

The question parents must ask and answer in their homes today is this: Have we cultivated an environment where anyone in the family can connect with God when they want to and in whatever way they want to? In other words, is God accessible in the temple? Or is God being drowned out by the din of technology, loud voices, and jumbled schedules?

If Jesus came to live with you, would he have to turn over some tables?

Building the House of God

Here are some practical ways to build a house of God. Obviously, creativity and individual circumstances can positively accentuate these.

Prayer. There is no greater lesson that parents can give their kids than modeling prayer. Praying before meals, absolutely. Praying at bedtime, yes. But also, teaching kids to pray at all times is important. The apostle Paul urged the Thessalonians to "pray continually."[5] Not just in times of need. But at all times.

Children need to see that prayer is more than a laundry list of "thank-yous" and "I need this" uttered at our bedsides. They need to see prayer as true conversation and fellowship with God. Pray in the car. Pray in the grocery store. Pray in the shower. Just as we talk to one another in all corners of the house, let our kids see that we can talk to God in all corners of his house, anytime.

Scripture tells us that Jesus longed to pray for children. When the disciples tried to stop parents from bringing their kids to him, Jesus told the disciples, "Let the little children come to me. Don't stop them!"[6] You can hear his tone, can't you? Anyone who earnestly seeks the Lord's favor is welcomed. I suspect that Jesus not only longed to pray for the children, but he also longed for them to see how praying is done.

In addition, ask your children to participate in your prayers. It feels less intimidating to know that Mom or Dad has already started the conversation with the unseen God. At first, simply ask them to share one-sentence prayers—for an ailing grandmother ("Please help Grandma get better") or an upcoming fear ("Please help me not to be nervous at the play this weekend"). Just getting them started is an important first step.

Listening to God is another important aspect of praying. Discovering that prayer is both talking and listening re-emphasizes the two-way communication channel. Ask your children what they hear about God in Bible stories or what they experience of him in nature or the world around them.[7]

Be sure to share answers to prayer. Let kids know when God has answered something you prayed about. "The earnest prayer of a righteous person has great power and wonderful results," said James.[8] Kids need to see that.

And when a prayer goes unanswered, don't hide your disappointment but point them to God's greater good at work. Helping kids know early on that God is not a short-order cook who hands out answers to every request is a good thing. God answers prayer *in God's way and time.*

A great visual lesson is to take a photograph or painting and cover up all of it except for a small square inch of color. Ask a child what they see. They may say "orange" or "a blob." But then pull back the cover and show them the full picture. That is how God works with us. We see the orange blob. He sees a Monet painting of wildflowers.

Bible study. Reading the Word together is very important because children are wired to ask questions. Be prepared: they will ask excellent questions. *How do you know God is talking to you? Why did Samson's hair hold all the power? Can you ever lose your Christianity?* Don't be afraid to say, "I don't know." While this may dent your pride a bit, it shows your children that life in the Bible never ends. We can read each day and learn something new.

Depending on the age of your child, choose an age-specific Bible. A four-year-old won't tune in to Numbers. The stories of Jonah and Samson? You bet. Dozens of children's Bibles are available on the market, many with kid-friendly study questions to help.

Try to find a regular time for daily devotionals. Kids thrive on routine, and building the Bible into your average day can be beneficial. Take time immediately after dinner, or perhaps before breakfast if you're not running late.

Bedtime is another good time, although parents need to make sure both they and the children are not too tired to concentrate.

Daily devotionals need not be extensive. Read a small passage, talk about it with your kids, and come up with ideas for implementing it. And depending on the passage, you can also build anticipation for upcoming passages. For example, read Daniel 2:1-13. Stopping at verse 13 is the equivalent of the television tactic of a black screen saying "To be continued . . ." Ask your kids: What do you think will happen? Will Daniel be caught and killed? What happens next?

Former Yale professor Randolph Crump Miller calls the Bible "a drama of redemption."[9] This helps teach it to all age levels as we see a living God at work in human relationships both in the past and even now.

Church. Restore church to a high priority. Help children understand that church is more than a building. Help them see the church as a family that gathers under God. Too many children go to church because their parents tell them they're going. Build an environment of participation. They belong to the church. They are the church.

One of the best habits to get into is to stop referencing the church altogether. Say "We are going to worship together" this morning instead of "We are going to church." The latter builds a concept that church only happens on Sunday morning. The church is a people of God on the go for the kingdom twenty-four seven. We don't *go* to church. We *are* the church. Everyday. Helping to change that nomenclature can change opinions too.

Ken Canfield suggests that the most important thing we can do is not *at* the service, but before and after.[10] Get the kids bathed and to bed on time on Saturday night.

Make sure you are ready in the morning so the family isn't rushed. And afterward, keep the family together for a while to discuss the sermon and the children's lesson. Probe what they think God enjoyed about the service.

Scripture quotes and memorization. Kids are sponges for memorizing things. I once heard a six-year-old at a camp site recite John 13 verbatim. The *entire* chapter. Now, admittedly, living out John 13 is more important than regurgitating it. But still, we need to take in these passages when we can.

Songs, flash cards, even some kids' videos are excellent at this.

Beyond rote memorization, be sure to look for modern-day examples of how these verses apply today. It's one thing to memorize that God is working for the good of those who love him.[11] It's another thing to see that truth in the life of a loved one who has since discovered that their recent financial hardship has led to a new God-honoring way of managing their money. Or an accident victim discovering the benefits of slowing down. God doesn't cause the trials or adversity, but he can use them for positive gain.

Talk with your children about God. The deepest questions I have ever been asked about faith and God have come from my kids. I think that's why Jesus enjoyed being around them so much. They didn't let theology or religion get in the way of thinking about God, and as a result, their insights and inquiries were free and often quite deep.

Bring God into your everyday conversations. When you see a sunrise, show your children that color of pink and orange that only God can create. I remember one afternoon picking up my son from kindergarten and telling him that we were stopping by the hospital to pray with a church family whose daughter was going in for outpatient surgery. At first, he griped about taking more time, but then I explained that we were being pastors that day, ministering to a fellow family in need. The idea of being a pastor caught his interest. I could see his mind swimming. *I can be a pastor, too?* As we approached the surgery waiting desk, the receptionist said, "Only clergy are allowed beyond this point." I said, "We are pastors from the church." She smiled at my son and then winked at me, "Oh, I didn't know you were pastors. Okay, *pastors,* come on through." My son still talks about that moment as he walked through those giant doors that said NO ENTRANCE. God opened those doors.

No greater passage of Scripture fits here than Deuteronomy 6:4-9:

> Hear, O Israel! The LORD is our God, the LORD alone. And you must love the LORD your God with all your heart, all your soul, and all your strength. And you must commit yourselves wholeheartedly to these commands I am giving you today. Repeat them again and again to your children. Talk about them when you are at home and when you are away on a journey, when you are lying down and when you are getting up again. Tie them to your hands as a reminder, and wear them on your forehead. Write them on the doorposts of your house and on your gates.

Did you notice to whom Moses was speaking? Parents. Family leaders. Repeat these commands to whom? Your children. How often? Continually. Talk about them where? Your home. Away from home. Make God your central theme.

The One Thing to Avoid

Building a house of God is easier than we think. One of the quickest ways to make it hard is to make it legalistic. Though I have given you some guidelines and suggestions on previous pages, you need not follow them each and every day. There will be days when you miss prayer or Bible study. God understands. What God doesn't want is for you to feel guilty, but God also wants your reasons for missing to be legitimate.

Constantly be looking for new ways to bring God into your lives. But if you want to make it difficult, then make it legalistic.

Jesus railed against legalism. He did not seek followers who felt they *had to* or *ought to* follow him. God has never wanted a coercive relationship. And kids are naturally wired to carry negative feelings toward anything forced upon them. "Because I said so" is not the reason why we pray or study the Bible with our children.

Be sure to give your house of God the breathing room for the unexpected and build an environment of celebration and inclusion. If you sense that prayer or Scripture reading has become rote and burdensome to your kids, change gears. Pick another time. Find another way.

A Sanctuary

Your home can be filled with God. Just look through the eyes of Christ and see what would happen if Jesus slept in the guest room tonight. He actually sleeps there every night anyway. It is now a matter of opening your eyes to see him and opening your heart to follow him.

Discussion Questions

1. What aspects of devotion and worship does your home struggle with? Prayer? Devotions? Why is that so?
2. Does your time with God feel forced? What are some creative ways to make your time feel more free and inviting for everyone?
3. How often do you talk about God with your children beyond Sunday morning? Reread Deuteronomy 6:6-9. What more does it say to you?
4. What if Jesus came over tonight? Think about what a night with Jesus might be like.

8
From Here to Eternity

Parenting doesn't end when a child turns eighteen. It definitely changes, but it doesn't stop. In fact, the goal of parenting goes far beyond the grave—the parent's or the child's. For what we do today matters not just in our hometown. It also matters in God's hometown also.

In this final chapter, we look at roles parents contribute to not only a child's future, but also their eternity.

New Jerusalem

The apostle Paul held a compelling perspective on his earthly life. Though he lived in a physical reality, his soul already walked in heaven. "But we are citizens of heaven, where the Lord Jesus Christ lives," Paul wrote to the Philippian church.[1] Paul didn't say that we *will* become citizens when we die, but that we who believe in Christ *are* citizens *right now*. This is why Paul claimed that he no longer lived, but instead, it was Jesus who lived inside of him.[2] The one who had ascended to God's right hand still remains among us. Heaven is closer than we think.

The apostle John said that we have already "crossed over," circumventing death to begin eternal life while here on earth.[3] You are not only a child of God; you also are a legal resident of his land.

Lynn Miller tells the story of filling out a passport

application. Where the form asked for his country of origin, Lynn wrote, "The Kingdom of God." The unsuspecting government employee wasn't sure how to process the information and eventually made Lynn resubmit the form with the "United States" clearly spelled out. Scripturally speaking, though, Lynn was correct.

No matter if your driver's license reads New Jersey, New York, or New Mexico. Your *true* residence is the New Jerusalem.

This truth was one of the driving forces of Paul's ministry, and it should be a driving force of every parent.

Beyond Here and Now

In his marching orders to the young pastor, Paul exhorts Timothy to "take hold of the eternal life" to which he was called.[4] Timothy's confession of Christ did not lead to an understanding about heaven. It brought heaven right to the heart that beat inside his chest.

In many ways, that is the same charge that God has given parents—to help their children open the door to heaven while still here on earth.

So how does our family life here on earth impact our eventual lives in heaven? How does our parenting have a bearing on our children's eventual homegoing to God? Can the temporal and eternal really be tied together? According to Paul and John, they become one saving faith in the Son.

Helping our children "take hold" of eternal life at an early age is a high order. Before we explore how to do this, some readers may be wondering why we need to do so. Doesn't God take it from there?

Heaven Can't Wait

Questions about heaven, even if not always spoken, have always been in our hearts. Gazing upon the "starry curtain,"[5] we have all pondered what lies beyond our street or cul-de-sac. We have all longed for a glimpse of the glorious life to come. We have held out hope that life on earth *isn't* all there is.

And when that day comes—when earth isn't all there is—what will become of us as spouses and parents? Will we still recognize and relate to one another? Will we still be lovers and mates? Will we still be Mom and Dad?

These are important questions. If the answer is "no," then the role of parenting is relegated to helping your child reach the finish line. If the answer is "yes," your role becomes breaking the tape *together* and continuing your relationship on the streets of gold.

Prolific author and researcher Randy Alcorn, who spent many years studying eternity for his book *Heaven,* says, "There's every reason to believe we'll pick right up in Heaven with relationships from Earth."[6] I will still be a husband and a dad in the life to come. Granted, Paul speaks of a new marriage in heaven between Christ and his bride, the church,[7] but that ever-present reality of being in union with Jesus only strengthens my experience as a spouse and dad. In other words, I will be a husband and father in heaven, but I will be one within the reality of being one with the Savior.

Alcorn says that "the notion that relationships with family will be lost in Heaven . . . is unbiblical. It denies the clear doctrine of continuity between this life and the next."[8] In other words, what I do as a father today will carry on into heaven. It certainly won't be the same as here on earth. But it won't be absent or unrecognizable either.

This may be a new concept for many readers, but being

a father or mother is an *eternal* responsibility. Once a parent, always a parent. Always. That is how important the role is to God. You continue to share it with God in the coming kingdom.

There are some parents who eagerly await their child's eighteenth birthday because all legal responsibilities for their physical welfare *technically* come to an end. For other parents, college graduation or simply moving out of the house begins a new phase of passive parenting from afar. *The hard part is over*, they sigh. *Now they're on their own.* There are other rites of passage too. But they all imply that your parenting identity begins to fade over time and eventually ceases at death.

But if we view parenting from an eternal perspective, we discover that our role is *reborn* in heaven. Even better is that there are no curfews, talking back, allowances, divorces, sickness, dysfunction, or lying. Best of all, Jesus is there too. For the first time, we get to experience parenthood in the pure light of unconditional, eternal love.

Your kids will still be your kids, but it will all be in the purview of being God's kids first.

Things Are Looking Up

Helping our children develop an eternity-focused life is the ultimate gift a parent can give. In particular are three lifelong benefits that can make a significant difference in your child's life.

Hope. Focusing on heaven keeps your child's eyes gazing above the fracas of this dying world. Seeing images of war, famine, and moral decay every day takes its toll on all of us. But if our children know something better awaits us, it firmly plants a living hope in our hearts—a hope to continue on while here on earth, and hopefully the desire to share that hope with someone who has lost it along the way.

This living hope, according to Peter, became readily available when Jesus left the tomb on Easter Sunday and is now "reserved" for every Christian.[9] Not reserved for heaven, but reserved to be experienced in power and truth right now.

Ironically, I am afraid of heights, especially open spaces such as mountaintops or Ferris wheels. Even glass elevators make my knees turn to jelly. There is a well-known solution that I try to employ when my willpower allows: Keep looking up. Look for the summit. Gaze at the clouds. Study the elevator's roof. But whatever you do, never look *down*.

An eternity-focused life passed on to our children is another way of saying: Keep looking up. The world will do all it can to entice them to look down into the abyss, and occasionally, they will take a peek. But if we know that everyone who "looks to the Son and believes in him shall have eternal life,"[10] we can find the strength, courage, and *hope* to carry on amid this broken world.

Anticipation. Paul was chained to a dungeon wall and yet rejoiced that his imprisonment was leading to many conversions.[11] Whether he made it out alive or not was not his concern because he was already a card-carrying member of God's kingdom. Frankly, Paul *looked forward* to leaving the earth.[12] He was eagerly anticipating the day. This is another benefit of an eternity-centered perspective.

One of my sons loves to ask questions about what heaven will be like. Will we be able to eat chocolate whenever we want to? Will there be a swing set? Will we be able to fly? Instead of answering him "Yes" or "No," I always push his imagination even farther into heaven with follow-up questions like "How would you fly? Would you soar high above everyone, or would you do loop-de-loops? What kind of chocolate? Do you think there would be a river of it like in *Charlie and the Chocolate Factory?*" If he wants to talk about heaven, we talk about heaven and then some.

The theology may get bypassed on occasion, but for young children, I'm more concerned that we build a healthy anticipation and preparedness for going there one day. Have you ever told one of your children about an upcoming vacation to Disney World or the Grand Canyon? For weeks, the conversation that gets repeated is, "How much longer? When do we leave? Can we ride the monorail? I want to ride the donkeys into the canyon. Are we flying?" They can't wait to get there. The thought of standing on the canyon ridge or walking past Cinderella's castle is on their minds every day. That's why if one of my kids wants to envision each of us soaring over rivers of milk chocolate, that's fine with me. I want him to *want* to go to heaven. Besides, I haven't completely given up on those chocolate rivers myself.

I tell my children often how excited I am about going to heaven one day. Sure, I temper those comments with how I am trusting in God's timing and cherishing every moment with them. In other words, I assure them that I don't plan on going *yet*. But I make sure they know that when God calls me home, you won't hear any groaning or pleas for a bit more time. Like Paul, I know it's a far better place, and I can't wait to be there.

The truth about death. Focusing on heaven also prepares children to better accept and understand death. It's not our favorite topic (nor theirs), but for Paul, being a citizen of heaven today makes death a bridge, not a jagged cliff. Chances are good that you will die before your children do. Whether that happens at an early age or later in life, letting your kids walk the streets of gold here on earth will prepare them for a greater hope when God calls you home. And eventually when it's their turn.

Most adults can recall the first funeral they attended as a child. The funeral home smelled strange and felt eerie. Familiar faces were unfamiliarly sad and sullen. And depending on your religious and family tradition, there may have been an open casket where the dead body was on display for those in mourning. That was the strangest sight of all.

At this point, the questions begin, although some kids are too afraid to ask them. This aspect of life is a stretch for even the most mature kids. Life is to be lived, not left behind. That's why how we respond is so critical. But I would argue that even more important is the foundation we have already laid in their young lives—that death is not the end, but the first step into heaven.

"If we are willing to explain simply and honestly what happens in death and give them a sense of assurance of life after death," says former Yale professor, Randolph Miller, "they can avoid the fears and superstitions that may be ruinous."[13]

Paul told the Corinthians that we live "in the face of death," but "the Good News" has resulted in eternal life nonetheless.[14] Why? Paul again has the answer. Our just payment for our sin is death, but God in his mercy extends a free gift to each of us—the gift of eternal life through Jesus.[15] We don't deserve it, but he gives it anyway.

To be certain, we should not sugarcoat death with our children. The hope of heaven is a far brighter light than death's darkness, and that should be our focus. But when death comes, we must accept it for what it is. As Randy Alcorn said, "Death is painful, and it's an enemy. But for those who know Jesus, death is the *final* pain and the *last* enemy."[16] That's the key: We can't romanticize heaven to the point of devaluing the suffering of death. We simply need to establish that the suffering of death is the death of suffering.

God alone. Another reason heaven is so important for kids to embrace is that it keeps the focus on God. When I believe there is more than just Mother Earth, I am most likely to live a life that impacts people beyond the here and now.

To say our society is self-centered and self-promotional is a little like calling a hurricane a shower. The me-first attitude of culture has slowly mutated into a me-only perspective for many. The only reason the rest of us are tolerated is in case we're needed for something.

But when children start seeing life as eternal, going beyond their driveway and school playground, children are able to expand not only their knowledge but also their hearts toward the higher things of God.

We need more people to think about others eternally because that means more people thinking beyond themselves and on God's purposes.

When It's All Said and Done

John said it best. "This is the way to have eternal life— to know you, the only true God, and Jesus Christ, the one you sent to earth."[17] Are we eager for our homegoing to heaven? Is it the living hope in our lives? Are we developing a home that *knows* God since that is the way to have eternal life?

No home is perfect. Never will a perfect home be here on earth. But that's why we need to keep pointing our children to the perfection of what lies beyond the earth. Perfection is not here.

In the end (which is actually the beginning), heaven will unite me, my spouse, my children, and my Savior. I can think of nothing more stirring to my soul. Until then, my earthly responsibilities remain to God, my wife, and my children—in that order.

Priority parenting means that one day my children and I can kneel together before God's throne. I long for that day.

Discussion Questions

1. What are your earliest recollections of heaven? What are your current thoughts about it?
2. How often have you talked with your children about heaven? What have you told them? What have they told you?
3. What are your children's experience(s) with death and dying? Have you talked about what death really leads to?
4. Have you considered your parenting role as an *eternal* role? How does that change your attitude and approach to parenting, knowing it will continue beyond the grave?

Afterword

It *is* happening. Slowly, but there is a movement afoot. Parents are beginning to slow down their hectic lifestyles and rebuild a meaningful home life. They are scrutinizing what extra-home activities their children join and carving out more free time for their children to be unchained from tight schedules and worldly expectations. They are discovering new ways of including God in their family conversations and activities. And there is a keen eye on heaven, trusting that we are travelers passing through this world. There is a Light at the end of life's tunnel.

I know this is happening because more parents are telling me. Some approach me like Nicodemus. They wait until the workshop has ended, and then double-checking that the room has emptied, they come to me with stories about the changes they are implementing in their homes. Some of their stories are heartbreaking, but change is never easy. Some stories are so uplifting that I wish I could broadcast them on the evening news.

Most of the stories, though, are shared by parents who are eager to encourage fellow parents about the freedom and joy that is found when God's priority is in order and Jesus is worshipped as the center of the universe. Like puzzle pieces finally fitting together, there is a natural flow to life that comes when God's priorities are honored.

Priority parenting doesn't guarantee that there won't be bumps in the home life. But it certainly empowers everyone to do what they do best—for parents to lead, for kids to learn and grow, and for God to be honored and followed.

I know these stories are still in a vast minority. The pressures of modern-day life on the average family are intense. But as Matthew 17:20 says, it only takes "faith as small as a mustard seed" to move a mountain. My hope is that this group of transformed parents can catch the ear of the throngs of other parents who are chasing the golden fleece, abandoning their leadership to their kids.

It's time to take the reins again. It's time to reign again. May you join the movement.

Notes

Preface

1. Federal Interagency Forum on Child and Family Statistics, *America's Children: Key National Indicators of Well-Being,* (Washington, D.C.: The Forum 2004).

Chapter 1. Heaven's Priority

1. Genesis 2:16-17.
2. Genesis 3:6.
3. Proverbs 3:12.
4. Ephesians 6:4.
5. Psalm 127:3.
6. Exodus 20:12, Proverbs 1:8; 4:1; Ephesians 6:1; Colossians 3:20.
7. Deuteronomy 6:2.
8. Exodus 20:3.
9. Kristyn Kusek, "They're Home. You're Not. Now What?" *Reader's Digest,* February 2005, 140.
10. U.S. Dept. of Labor, Bureau of Labor Statistics, "Families by Presence and Relationship of Employed Members and Family Type," 2002-3 annual averages.
11. Juliet B. Schor, *The Overworked American: The Unexpected Decline of Leisure* (New York: Basic Books, 1991); cited by the Center for Work and Family. Online: www.centerforworkand family.com.
12. Brennan Manning and Jim Hancock, *Posers, Fakers, and Wannabes: Unmasking the Real You* (Colorado Springs: NavPress, 2003).
13. Talking with Teens: The YMCA Parent and Teen Survey Final Report. Online: www.ymca.net

14. Betty M. Caldwell, *In Support of Families*, ed. Michael W. Yogman and T. Berry Brazelton (Cambridge, Mass.: Harvard University Press, 1986), chapter 13.

15. Proverbs 22:6.

16. James U. McNeal, *The Kids Market: Myth and Realities* (Ithaca, N.Y.: Paramount Market Publishing 1999), 78.

17. Nathan Dungan, *Prodigal Sons, Material Girls: How Not to Be Your Child's ATM* (Hoboken, N.J.: Wiley & Sons, 2003), 26.

18. Hebrews 12:11.

19. Proverbs 3:12.

20. Lewis Grant, cited by John Ortberg in *The Life You've Always Wanted* (Downers Grove, Ill.: InterVarsity Press, 1997).

21. Interview by Lisa Jackson, "Kiss Guilt Goodbye," *Christian Parenting Today* 11, no. 7 (Sept./Oct. 1999): 446.

22. Second Corinthians 5:17.

23. Matthew 19:26.

Chapter 2. Homesick

1. U.S. Census Bureau, "Housing Vacancies and Home Ownership," Annual Statistics: 2004. Online: www.census.gov.

2. *The Columbia World of Quotations* (New York: Columbia University Press, 1996). Online: www.bartleby.com/66/.

3. Acts 3:25.

4. Second Corinthians 5:1.

5. William Doherty and Barbara Carlson, "Overscheduled Kids, Underconnected Families," in *Take Back Your Time*, ed. by John deGraff (San Francisco: Bartlett-Koehler 2003), 41.

6. Sharon Vandivere, Kathryn Tout, Martha Zaslow, Julia Calkins, and Jeffrey Capizzano, "Unsupervised Time: Family and Child Factors Associated with Self-Care," *Occasional Paper* 71 (November 2003). Online: www.urban.org.

7. John F. O'Grady, *Jesus, Lord, and Christ* (New York: Paulist Press 1973), 81.

8. Cynthia Langham, University of Detroit study, 1992.

9. John 1:2-3.

10. Ephesians 1:9.

11. Hebrews 13:8.

12. Revelation 1:8; 21:6; 22:13.

13. Max Lucado, *It's Not About Me: Rescue from the Life We Thought Would Make Us Happy* (Brentwood, Tenn.: Integrity Publishers, 2004).

14. John P. Murray, *Using TV Sensibly: Children and Television* (Manhattan, Kan.: Kansas State University, 1995).

Chapter 3. There's a Spouse in the House

1. Genesis 2:24b.

2. Hebrews 13:4.

3. Isaiah 54:5.

4. Ken R. Canfield, *The Seven Secrets of Effective Fathers* (Carol Stream, Ill.: Tyndale, 2001), 133.

5. Brian and Deborah Newman, Frank and Mary Alice Minirth, and Robert and Susan Hemfelt, *Passages of Marriage: Five Growth Stages That Will Take Your Marriage to Greater Intimacy and Fulfillment* (Nashville: Thomas Nelson, 1991), 109.

6. Bob Moeller, "Marriage's Best Gift," *Marriage Partnership*, Winter 1998.

7. Ephesians 5:25.

8. Scott Stanley et al., *A Lasting Promise: A Christian Guide to Fight for Your Marriage* (San Francisco: Jossey-Bass, 1998), 264-70.

9. Bill Cosby, *Fatherhood* (New York: Bantam Books, 1986), chapter 1.

10. Psalm 34:11.

11. Canfield, *Seven Secrets*, 190.

12. John MacArthur, *Different by Design* (Colorado Springs: Victor Publishing, 1994).

Chapter 4. Kids Will Say No

1. Cathy Lynn Grossman, "Keeping the Faith Kept Gunman's Captive Safe," *USA Today*, March 15, 2005.

2. Richard Swenson, *Margin: The Overload Syndrome* (Colorado Springs: NavPress, 2002), 123.

3. John Ortberg, *The Life You've Always Wanted* (Downers Grove, Ill.: InterVarsity Press, 1997).

4. Steve Ganger, *Time Warped: First Century Time Stewardship for 21st Century Living* (Scottdale, Pa.: Herald Press, 2004), 26.

5. Luke 10:38-42.

6. Philippians 2:3.

7. John 4:10.

8. Christine Sine, *Sacred Rhythms: Finding a Peaceful Pace in a Hectic World* (Grand Rapids: Baker Books, 2003), 26.

9. Pamela Evans. *The Overcommitted Christian: Serving God Without Wearing Out* (Downers Grove, Ill.: InterVarsity, 2001).

Chapter 5. Nobody's Home

1. Online: www.foxnews.com, July 15, 2005.

2. Online: www.cnn.com, " 'Hockey Dad' Gets 6 to 10 Years for Fatal Beating," January 25, 2005.

3. Seth Davis, "All About Me." Online: www.sports illustrated.cnn.com, July 9, 2005.

4. C. V. Nevius. "There Are Big Problems and Ready Solutions: The Cost of High Stakes on Little League Games," *San Francisco Chronicle*, December 11, 2000.

5. Ibid.

6. Little League Baseball and Softball 2005 Media Guide.

7. U.S. Youth Soccer 2005 Media Kit.

8. Boy Scouts of America Fact Sheet. Online: www. scouting.org.

9. David Elkind, *Ties That Stress: The New Family Imbalance* (Cambridge, Mass.: Harvard University Press, 1995), chapter 6.

10. David Elkind, *The Hurried Child: Growing Up Too Fast Too Soon*, 3d ed. (New York: Perseus, 2001), 31.

11. Cited in Dave Murphy, "Stressed Out," *San Francisco Chronicle*, May 8, 2005.

12. Elkind, *Hurried Child*, 32.

13. Michael and Diane Medved, *Saving Childhood: Protecting Our Children from the National Assault on Innocence* (New York: HarperCollins, 1998), 180.

14. William Doherty and Barbara Carlson, "Overscheduled Kids, Underconnected Families," in *Take Back Your Time*, ed. John deGraff (San Francisco: Bartlett-Koehler, 2003), 44.

15. Matthew 11:28.

Chapter 6. Send in the Clouds

1. Cited by Sonja Lewis, "Protective Parents, Busy Schedules Leave Children Little Time to Savor Season," *Atlanta Journal-Consitution*, June 28, 2002.

2. Online: www.commercialalert.org.

3. "Understanding the Impact of Media on Childen and Teens," American Academy of Pediatrics. Online: www.aap.org.

4. Cited by William Doherty and Barbara Carlson, "Overscheduled Kids, Underconnected Families," in *Take Back Your Time*, ed. John deGraff (San Francisco: Bartlett-Koehler, 2003), 40; and Betsy Taylor, "Recapturing Childhood," in *Take Back Your Time*, 47.

5. "Slowing Down the After-School Schedule," National Association of Children's Hospitals. Online: www.childrens hospitals.net.

6. Penelope Leach, *Children First* (New York: Knopf, 1994), 103.

7. Abraham and Dorothy Schmitt, *Renewing Family Life* (Scottdale, Pa.: Herald Press, 1985), 69.

8. Marie Sherlock, *Living Simply with Children* (New York: Three Rivers Press, 2003), 191-200.

Chapter 7. The House of God

1. Luke 10:42, NCV.

2. These statistics are cited by the National Sleep Foundation and its *Sleep in America* surveys. Online: www.sleep foundation.org.

3. John Ortberg and Ruth Haley Barton, *An Ordinary Day with Jesus: Leader's Guide* (Grand Rapids: Zondervan, 2000), x.

4. Mark 11:17, NKJV.

5. First Thessalonians 5:17, NIV.

6. Matthew 19:14.

7. Marlene Kropf, *Mennonite Brethren Herald* 37:3.

8. James 5:16.

9. Randolph Crump Miller, *Your Child's Religion* (Garden City, N.Y.: Doubleday, 1962), 119.

10. Ken R. Canfield, *The Seven Secrets of Effective Fathers* (Carol Stream, Ill.: Tyndale, 2001), 198.

11. Romans 8:28.

Chapter 8. From Here to Eternity

1. Philippians 3:20.

2. Galatians 2:20.

3. John 5:24, NIV.

4. First Timothy 6:12, NIV.

5. Psalm 104:2b.

6. Randy Alcorn, *Heaven* (Carol Stream, Ill.: Tyndale, 2004), 337.

7. Ephesians 5:31-32.

8. Alcorn, *Heaven*, 337.

9. First Peter 1:4, NKJV.

10. John 6:40, NIV.

11. Philippians 1:12-14.

12. Philippians 1:20-23.

13. Randolph Crump Miller, *Your Child's Religion* (Garden City, N.Y.: Doubleday 1962), 126.

14. Second Corinthians 2:14-16.

15. Romans 6:23.

16. Alcorn, *Heaven*, 451.

17. John 17:3.

Bibliography

Alcorn, Randy. *Heaven*. Carol Stream, Ill.: Tyndale, 2004.

Canfield, Ken R. *The Seven Secrets of Effective Fathers*. Carol Stream, Ill.: Tyndale, 2001.

Cosby, Bill. *Fatherhood*. New York: Bantam Books, 1986.

Doherty, William, and Barbara Carlson. "Overscheduled Kids, Underconnected Families." In *Take Back Your Time*. Edited by John deGraff. San Francisco: Bartlett-Koehler, 2003.

Dungan, Nathan. *Prodigal Sons, Material Girls: How Not to Be Your Child's ATM*. Hoboken, N.J.: Wiley & Sons, 2003.

Elkind, David. *The Hurried Child: Growing Up Too Fast Too Soon*. 3d ed. New York: Perseus, 2001.

———. *Ties That Stress: The New Family Imbalance*. Cambridge, Mass.: Harvard University Press, 1995.

Evans, Pamela. *The Overcommitted Christian: Serving God Without Wearing Out*. Downers Grove, Ill.: InterVarsity, 2001.

Ganger, Steve. *Time Warped: First Century Time Stewardship for 21st Century Living*. Scottdale, Pa.: Herald Press, 2004.

Leach, Penelope. *Children First*. New York: Knopf, 1994.

MacArthur, John. *Different by Design*. Colorado Springs: Victor Publishing, 1994.

Manning, Brennan, and Jim Hancock. *Posers, Fakers, and Wannabes: Unmasking the Real You*. Colorado Springs: NavPress, 2003.

McNeal, James U. *The Kids Market: Myth and Realities*. Ithaca, N.Y.: Paramount Market Publishing 1999.

Medved, Michael, and Diane Medved. *Saving Childhood: Protecting Our Children from the National Assault on Innocence*. New York: HarperCollins, 1998.

Miller, Randolph Crump. *Your Child's Religion*. Garden City, N.Y.: Doubleday 1962.

Newman, Brian, and Deborah Newman, et al. *Passages of Marriage: Five Growth Stages That Will Take Your Marriage to Greater Intimacy and Fulfillment*. Nashville: Thomas Nelson, 1991.

Ortberg, John. *The Life You've Always Wanted*. Downers Grove, Ill.: InterVarsity Press, 1997.

Ortberg, John, and Ruth Haley Barton. *An Ordinary Day with Jesus: Leader's Guide*. Grand Rapids: Zondervan, 2000.

Rosenfeld, Alvin A., and Nicole Wise. *The Over-Scheduled Child: Avoiding the Hyper-Parenting Trap*. New York: St. Martin's Press, 2001.

Schmitt, Abraham, and Dorothy Schmitt. *Renewing Family Life*. Scottdale, Pa.: Herald Press, 1985.

Schor, Juliet B. *The Overworked American: The Unexpected Decline of Leisure*. New York: Basic Books, 1991.

Sherlock, Marie. *Living Simply with Children*. New York: Three Rivers Press, 2003.

Sine, Christine. *Sacred Rhythms: Finding a Peaceful Pace in a Hectic World*. Grand Rapids: Baker Books, 2003.

Stanley, Scott, et al. *A Lasting Promise: A Christian Guide to Fight for Your Marriage*. San Francisco: Jossey-Bass, 1998.

Swenson, Richard. *Margin, the Overload Syndrome*. Colorado Springs: NavPress, 2002.

Taylor, Betsy. "Recapturing Childhood." In *Take Back Your Time*. Edited by John deGraff. San Francisco: Bartlett-Koehler, 2003.

Yogman, Michael W,. and T. Berry Brazelton, eds. *In Support of Families*. Cambridge, Mass.: Harvard University Press, 1986.